Amy and Julie Zhang

# THE DUMPLING SISTERS COOKBOOK

Over 100 favourite recipes from a Chinese family kitchen

For Pei Wen, Maria, and Justin
'Wei, lei sic joh fan mei ah?'
'喂, 你食咗饭未呀?'

# CONTENTS

**Hi there. We're Amy and Julie.** We're sisters, keen home cooks and (95 per cent of the time) best friends. We grew up in beautiful New Zealand and that is where our food story begins.

At the very centre of that story is family. For over two decades of dewy Sunday mornings, our family has been piling into Dad's temperamental old van. It's usually five slightly groggy people in the front and a serious game of Tetris in the back: big white buckets of fresh ingredients, jumbo dried noodle nests and plenty of soy sauce – all neatly and securely stacked to ensure that the short journey to the market doesn't end in a premature stir-fry. Towing behind the van is our rickety food cart, which has become much more than a space for selling. It's a stage for Mum and Dad to showcase their amazing cooking skills, an adored fixture at the Riccarton Rotary Sunday Market in Christchurch, and an honorary member of our family. The cart at stall number 'A25' represents the centre of a much larger family, too, for it is where our customers have seen us and our little brother Justin grow into adults.

It was the combination of setting up shop at the market and being immersed in a home where food meant family that taught us how to cook and eat. It's no wonder that our fondest childhood memories are inextricably connected with food: from nightly dinners at a table lovingly adorned with colourful sharing dishes, to road trips with delicious soy chicken packed in the chilly bin.

Although we were oceans away from China, Mum and Dad's creativity in the kitchen gave us a taste of their childhoods. And what a fabulous team they are: Dad is the deep-frying and marinating expert, while Mum's (all five feet of her) ability to toss an Everest of noodles in a wok never ceases to amaze. They made eager students (and taste testers) of us and we absorbed every lesson.

In recent years, the same hunger for learning brought us to the other side of the world, to study subjects far removed from food: Amy for a chemistry PhD at Cambridge and Julie a criminology Masters at Oxford. We finished our degrees at around the same time, and from the closing of one chapter sprung a mutual urge to go back to our food roots – and so The Dumpling Sisters was born.

We knew that for a lot of people, making Chinese food at home, especially dumplings, might seem daunting or mysterious. So we set up a blog and made YouTube videos dedicated to sharing what we know and love about Chinese food. Although it was terrifying and awkward to see ourselves on film at the beginning, we had a hunch that our encouraging video tutorials could help home cooks feel more confident about cooking our recipes. Above all, the videos are an invitation to cook along with us in our kitchen: anytime, anywhere.

In the first few months family and friends were our loyal (and only!) followers so when we received the first photos of our food recreated in home kitchens all over the world it was truly heart-warming. Fast-forward to today and we are still sharing our favourite recipes online; recipes that are drawn from the unwritten Cantonese cookbook that was so central to our upbringing.

Our recipes have always been the heartland of what we do, so when the idea of writing a cookbook was floated we could hardly wait to jump right in. This cookbook is dedicated to every long-time fan of Chinese food, and the newly curious.

We would love for these pages to become dog-eared and splattered with all manner of sauces and seasonings as you cook your way through the chapters that represent different ways to enjoy Chinese food. We have got pretty dim sum, fuss-free meals, traditional family-style eating, a major noodle-fest, dishes fit for a proper feast, and moreish baked goods, too. And like all good things this one ends with dessert, namely a selection of terrific Chinese desserts – something that we hope will convince you that the Chinese can do great sweet things too.

At its very heart, *The Dumpling Sisters Cookbook* is an invitation to cook alongside us so you too can learn by doing, just as we did at Mum and Dad's side.

With that, we wish you happy cooking – and even happier eating.

A&J x

# KNOW YOUR 'MOUTHFEELS'

The Chinese revere textures and sensations in the mouth just as much as they do flavour. This is not highbrow stuff; it is simply a part of the eating experience. By extension, *hau gum* (literally, 'mouthfeel') is a part of our everyday language, peppering our dinner conversations with appreciative murmurs of how satisfyingly *faa, lum* and so on certain dishes are. Because there isn't always an equivalent English term for the various categories of mouthfeel, we have tried our best to describe our favourite textures and sensations below. Our list is not exhaustive, but these mouthfeels are among the most common. Draw from them the next time you eat something with a particularly enjoyable or surprising texture and soon you too will be dropping the terms during meals with friends and family.

### FAA

*Faa* foods are usually rich and 'melt in the mouth'. They are sometimes even delicate enough to collapse at the slightest touch of your tongue. Think chocolate mousse, fluffy, buttery mash and crumbly shortbread. Try the potatoes in our Potato and Chicken Curry (page 116) and the pastry in our Pineapple Tarts (page 215) for some serious *faa* action.

### (BOK BOK) CHEOW

The onomatopoeic name of this one gives it away: *cheow* is anything with great crunch, and adding the prefix *bok bok* means that something is super-*cheow*. For example, roast pork crackling and filo pastry are at their finest when they are *cheow*. The same goes for Crispy Noodle Nests (page 178), Golden Spring Rolls (page 28) and Peanut and Sesame Brittle (page 239).

### SONG

Food is *song* when it has a refreshingly crisp bite, like coming across a piece of cucumber in a leafy salad. Other *song* foods include tender calamari, the flesh of lychees and fresh watermelon. Some of our favourite *song* recipes include our Stir-fried Cucumber (page 138), Spicy Squid Stir-fry (page 107) and Prawn Claw Dumplings (page 25).

### SOUNG

These foods readily crumble or flake when you bite into them because they have a loose and airy structure. Puff pastry and deep-fried prawn crackers are delicious examples, as are Sweet and Salty Walnut Cookies (page 219), Custard Egg Tarts (page 232) and Flaky Red Bean Pastries (page 226).

### WAAT

As one of the most sought-after mouthfeels in Chinese cooking, *waat* foods are silky, slippery and smooth. They also tend to be moist; think fruit jelly, mangoes and perfectly ripe avocados. In Cantonese cooking, marinating meat with bicarbonate of soda and cornflour helps to make it more *waat*. Achieving the *waat* texture makes or breaks dishes like Whole Steamed Fish (page 108), Silky Steamed Eggs (page 99) and Ginger Milk Pudding (page 255).

### DAAN NGAA

This means 'springy teeth', so foods with this quality bounce against your bite as you sink your teeth into them. Turkish delight does the trick, as do the Aromatic Steamed Beef Meatballs (page 130) and springy fish balls in Hokkien Noodles (page 169).

## YEE UN

These foods are satisfyingly chewy. It takes a bit more work to eat them, but this doesn't mean that *yee un* foods are unpleasant or tough. For example, al dente pasta and chewy buttermilk crumpets are immensely satisfying to chomp through, as are the Spring Onion Pancakes (page 55), Sweet Sticky-filled Pancakes (page 242) and *kansui* (alkaline water) wonton noodles in Fried Sauce Noodles (page 171).

## MEEN

In Cantonese, *meen* means pillowy and soft. For example, *meen toi* is a duvet inner and *meen fa tong* are fluffy marshmallows. The cloud-like bun wrapper of Steamed Pork Buns (page 40) and the fine spongy crumb of Mum and Dad's Vibrant Pandan Cake (page 230) demonstrate the *meen* mouthfeel.

## LUM

*Lum* means soft and velvety, like what you would expect from a brilliant bread and butter pudding or an ultra-moist self-saucing chocolate cake. It also describes meat that 'falls off the bone', such as slow-cooked pulled pork and lamb shanks. The carrot logs in Watercress Soup (page 90) become incredibly *lum* after many hours in the pot, as does the meat in Chicken and Parsnip Soup (page 93).

## MAA LAAT

Although this one is not usually associated with Cantonese cooking, it is one of our favourites and also one of the most interesting sensations to experience for the first time. *Maa laat* means 'numbing spiciness'. It is achieved through the use of Sichuan peppercorns, making this mouthfeel one of the hallmarks of Sichuanese cooking. Mapo Tofu (page 100) is the most popular *maa laat* dish worldwide, while lesser-known dishes like Spicy Blistered Beans (page 146) and 'Fish Fragrant' Aubergine (page 145) also deliver a uniquely *maa laat* punch.

# 10 TIPS & TRICKS

While there's no magic dust needed to cook delicious Chinese food, there are some tips and tricks you can use to make the result seem magical. Here are our top ten picks: think of them as rules of thumb that a little Chinese granny would pass down to you, as Mum and Dad did to us.

### 1 THE MAGIC OF BICARBONATE OF SODA

The secret to creating the melt-in-your-mouth texture of meats in Chinese food is bicarbonate of soda. We almost always include a few pinches in our marinades because it relaxes the tightly wound ropes of protein in tough muscle meat that give your jaw a workout. It transforms even the toughest of meats, which means you can use cheaper cuts.

### 2 SLICING MEAT 'AGAINST THE GRAIN'

Slicing meat (especially beef) 'against the grain' is a neat trick for tenderising meats even further. Simply have a good look at the meat and figure out what direction the fibres are running in (this is the 'grain'), and then slice at right angles to, or 'against', this grain. You can think of the fibres as a thick bundle of elastic cords – the shorter the cords are, the less work your jaw has to do.

### 3 VELVETY CORNFLOUR

Coating meats in cornflour before cooking locks in the juices and creates a wonderfully *waat* (silky, velvety) mouthfeel. We add a teaspoon or two to our marinades. Cornflour is also behind those thick, glossy sauces in Chinese food (it's not oil!). Toward the end of cooking, mix in a slurry of cornflour and water and watch as a lush, glistening and translucent sauce clings to every ingredient as the cornflour cooks through.

### 4 SOY SAUCE: LIGHT VS DARK

Light soy sauce packs a saltier punch than its darker sibling so we use it primarily for flavouring and seasoning. The intense liquorice hue of dark soy sauce, on the other hand, is ideal for adding colour to dishes such as fried rice and noodles. Its syrupy, almost caramel-like quality in both consistency and taste is also great for adding richness and body to braises. Check out the glossary of ingredients on page 259 for how to pick the best dark soy, for they vary greatly in quality.

### 5 LINGERING SESAME

We can never resist the seductive nutty aroma of toasted sesame oil. To allow its qualities to shine through, we avoid using it as a cooking oil as its delicate fragrance is destroyed by intense heat. Instead, we suggest using it sparingly as a flavour enhancer at the end of cooking.

### 6 HOT WATER DUMPLING DOUGH

To create the most pliable, robust and easy to handle dumpling dough, we make ours using hot water rather than cold. This partially cooks the flour and creates resilient dough that can be shaped, rolled out thinly, and manipulated to create beautiful pleats.

### 7 GARLIC + PORK

The Chinese are well known for adoring pork but sometimes it has an uninviting smell (called boar taint) when cooked, especially when steamed. Our antidote is simple: add garlic – with a slightly heavier hand than usual – and cook like normal.

### 8 GINGER + FISH

The awakening zing of ginger does a fabulous job of cutting through fishiness and we use it with even the freshest of fish to enhance its natural sweetness. Consider cutting the ginger into long, thin tendrils that imitate swaying swathes of seagrass.

## 9 STEAMING

Steam has a wonderful ability to coax flavours out of the simplest of ingredients. Mum never used a fancy bamboo steamer when we were growing up, and you don't need to either. Simply choose a steaming dish that fits inside a lidded saucepan or wok, raise the dish above the base of the pan (a steaming rack, or an upright bowl will do), and fill your pan with boiling water to a level just below where the base of the dish will be. It is best to use a steam-proof dish such as enamel, Pyrex or everyday china. When steaming meat, we use about 50 per cent more cornflour (to mop up the juices that are released during steaming) and omit the bicarbonate of soda (as it will froth up).

## 10 LOVE YOUR WOK

**Let's start with the cooking vessel.** A carbon steel wok is best for home stir-frying, but you can make do with a large frying pan with high sides – just choose something that will give the ingredients plenty of room to move around in as you stir and fry. The beauty of a carbon steel wok (very cheap at Chinese supermarkets) is that its thin walls transfer heat quickly, which is crucial for creating the characteristic heat-kissed smokiness of stir-fried food. For a no-fuss cooking experience, go for a wok with a long wooden handle (rather than two ear-shaped handles at opposite sides) and a flat (as opposed to curved) base that will sit unsupported on home hobs.

**Getting the wok ready.** New carbon steel woks need to be prepared or 'seasoned' for cooking. Begin by scrubbing the wok well with hot soapy water to remove the anti-rust oil coating, then give it a quick wipe. Dry thoroughly over a low heat and then replace the protective coating by smearing the inside surface with a thin film of cooking oil (kitchen paper is handy here).

**When you are ready to cook.** Have all the ingredients prepped, including the cornflour slurry if using (see above). If you are using a wok, it should be extremely hot before you add the oil, which is immediately followed by your first ingredient (often aromatics like garlic and ginger). When stir-frying, we use a range of motions: stir, turn, flip, toss (!) – using two spatulas if it helps. In restaurants, the food is usually in constant motion because you don't want it to catch over the intense heat. At home, you will find that you will need to leave the ingredients alone for a while to give them a chance to cook through, or for meats to develop a caramel crust. To ensure thorough cooking, sprinkle in some water and cover with a lid – this will create steam that helps to deliver heat to the core of the ingredients. Alternatively, blanch your vegetables beforehand.

**Cleaning? There's an art to that too.** A steel wok loves a bit of TLC so when it's done its duty, scrub well in hot water, but don't be tempted to use detergent as this will strip away the protective oil coating. Then dry as above (wipe, then heat), before using kitchen paper to reapply a thin film of oil. Over multiple uses, a well-seasoned wok essentially acts as a non-stick surface so it's worth doing these extra steps. Think of it as buffing a vintage car or a pair of designer patent heels – it will be a joy to own and use for many years.

# ADD AN EXOTIC

We may have let out a delighted squeal or two when we spotted canned water chestnuts in the international aisle of our local supermarket. It was something of a light bulb moment for us: people are enthusiastic about experimenting with new ingredients.

To do our bit for the evolving global palate, we have included a nifty feature called 'add an exotic' 🪷 . These optional extras appear in some recipes and are Chinese ingredients that probably feel unfamiliar at the moment. But whether an 'exotic' adds an interesting mouthfeel or greater depth of flavour, it can take a Chinese dish from pretty darn good to downright sublime. Our hope is that eventually these ingredients will no longer seem 'exotic' as they become a natural part of your cooking repertoire, utilised with the same level of comfort and frequency as pak choi or soy sauce. We are looking forward to the day when fermented beancurd pops up in local supermarkets, but in the meantime all of these ingredients are readily available at good Chinese supermarkets.

### GUM CHOI (GOLDEN NEEDLE VEGETABLE) 金针菜

These spindly golden yellow needles are not vegetables at all, but the edible flower petals of the daylily plant. Purchase them in dried form, then simply steep the needles in warm water before cooking so they become plump and juicy. The best way to seal in the delicately fragrant flavour of *gum choi* is by steaming them alongside ingredients that will happily take on the subtle perfume of the needles, such as chicken thighs. [1]

### MOOK YEE (WOOD EAR MUSHROOMS) 木耳

What starts out as featherlight dried petals rapidly blossoms into lush and juicy blooms after rehydration in water. *Mook yee* is usually added to dishes to take advantage of its *song* (refreshingly crisp) mouthfeel (page 8). It is also a wonderful vehicle for flavour because sauces and seasonings get caught within its cloud-like pleats. Another common variety, *wun yee* (cloud ear) is similarly *song* and pleated. [2]

### HARM YU (SALTED PRESERVED FISH) 咸鱼

Just a few precious nuggets of this powerhouse ingredient will send you straight to the seaside. Keep an eye out for the *muoi houng* variety if you can – this means that the fish has a *faa* (melt-in-the-mouth) mouthfeel (page 8). The other variety, *sut yook harm yu* literally translates as 'hard-fleshed salted fish'. [3]

### JI JOOK (DRIED BEAN CURD) 支竹

Dried bean curd, also known as 'tofu skin', is a by-product of soy milk production: as the milk boils, a robust skin forms on the surface, which is later skimmed off in sheets, dried out, and rehydrated for cooking. Though by itself *ji jook* lacks a distinctive flavour, its brilliantly wrinkly surface is perfect for mopping up flavoursome sauces. When cooked slowly, as in stews, *ji jook* becomes very tender to the bite. [4]

## KONG YU CHU (DRIED SCALLOPS) 江瑶柱

These dark caramel-coloured nuggets are seriously pungent and rich in umami flavour, making them prized in Chinese cooking. Rehydrate them in water before using them sparingly – it only takes a little for the distinctive flavour to shine through. [5]

## LARP CHEONG (CHINESE SAUSAGE) 腊肠

This is a dried pork sausage with sweet undertones and a waxy texture ('larp' refers to the waxiness). Sliced or diced larp cheong is brilliant either steamed or stir-fried to render out the moreish flavour from the fatty bit. [6]

## JA CHOI (PRESERVED MUSTARD STEM) 榨菜

The funny knobbly appearance of whole ja choi belies a fantastic little ingredient that is perfectly salty, sour and spicy all at once. Ja choi has a song (refreshingly crisp) mouthfeel, and if you love pickled dill, you will be an instant fan of preserved mustard stem too. Chop it up and use it as a condiment for Silken Congee (page 26), or as a flavoursome addition to soups and sauces, or serve as an accompaniment for steamed meat dishes. You can purchase ja choi in several different forms, but our favourite varieties are sold as foil-wrapped sachets for convenient single servings or whole bulbs in cans. If you are using whole ja choi, rinse the stems before chopping them to remove any grittiness. [7]

## HARM SHURN CHOI (PICKLED MUSTARD GREENS) 酸菜

Pungent, sharp, and addictively sour, harm shurn choi (literally, salty sour vegetable) are handy to keep in the cupboard for adding the zing factor to soups and stir-fries. They are available in clear plastic packets at Chinese supermarkets, but if you have access to fresh mustard greens you can pickle them yourself, too. Simply pop the greens into a clean and sterilised jar together with some vinegar, salt and sugar, then cover and refrigerate for at least three days before serving. [8]

## HAR MEY (DRIED SHRIMP) 虾米

Widely used for its ability to impart a unique umami aroma to a variety of dishes, har mey are often rehydrated in water before cooking. We also like to fry them into crispy savoury morsels for sprinkling on top of salads. [9]

## FOUR YU/NARM YU (WHITE/RED FERMENTED BEANCURD) 腐乳/南乳

Four yu (white fermented beancurd) and narm yu (red fermented beancurd) are dainty beancurd bricks with a texture that is similar to creamy blue cheese. The flavour comes from the liquid in which the tofu is brined, resulting in a salty, slightly tangy and sometimes spicy profile. Narm yu is distinctively different to four yu due to the addition of red yeast rice. Simply mash up the beancurd before adding it to stir-fries and sauces. For the ultimate pared-down supper, sprinkle granulated sugar on top of a single brick then use the tip of your chopsticks to gradually nip away at it as you wolf down a bowl of rice. [10]

yum cha

The air-conditioning whirrs loudly to keep the heaving room cool, yet its efforts are drowned out by a blanket of noisy gossip. Mismatched tableware is cleared and re-set at an impossible speed and a team of no-nonsense waitresses expertly weave their trolleys through the maze of tightly packed tables. They tempt diners with cheeky peeks inside stacks of bamboo steamers, while oven-baked and deep-fried goodies are proudly proffered in full display: golden-brown morsels arranged in sets of three. Tea is poured and teapot lids are left ajar to signal for refills. Food is critiqued, plates are polished off, and the bill fought over – sometimes rather ferociously!

This is the chaotic but much-treasured scene of *yum cha*, a Cantonese dining tradition with a name that literally means 'drink tea'. Think of it as the Chinese version of small-plates eating, like Spanish tapas or an English morning tea. In our family, *yum cha* has always been a treat. Whether we are deciding at the last minute to visit our local on a rainy Sunday (meaning we can't set up shop ourselves at the market) or meeting our extended family at incredible *yum cha* restaurants in Guangzhou, there is always an air of excitement about the prospect of partaking in the brilliant food and cleansing tea.

Having dubbed ourselves 'The Dumpling Sisters', this chapter is particularly dear to us because it is home to our namesake: a sumptuous selection of gorgeous handmade dumplings. But that's not all. We have also developed DIY dim sum (literally, 'to touch the heart') recipes for plenty of other *yum cha* favourites too. We hope that you have fun creating these little edible works of art – some will take extra practice to perfect, but they are all 100 per cent worth the effort.

These golden bite-sized morsels are our little brother Justin's absolute favourite, and also one of the most popular dim sum worldwide. The literal translation of *siu mai* is 'cook sell' – a nod to the practice of these juicy dumplings being rapidly made and sold as tantalising street food. It's definitely worth the extra effort to mince your own pork loin or shoulder as it makes for a much juicier bite, but pork mince will also work.

# pork and prawn open dumplings

1. Soak the Chinese mushrooms in a bowl of hot water with the sugar for 30 minutes, then drain. Remove and discard the stalks and finely dice the caps.

2. If using pork loin or shoulder, cut it into 1cm cubes, keeping the fat on. Then use a heavy knife or a cleaver to *dhuk* it, meaning to repeatedly chop through the pork with force until it resembles coarse mince.

3. Put the pork and all the marinade ingredients including 1 tablespoon water into a large bowl, then use a pair of chopsticks to vigorously stir in one direction (e.g. clockwise) until the meat binds to itself. Cover and chill for at least 30 minutes. Gently stir the mushrooms and prawns into the marinated pork.

4. If you are using wonton wrappers, use a 9cm cookie cutter to cut these into rounds. To wrap the *siu mai*, put 1 tablespoon of the filling into the centre of a wrapper. Use the handle of the spoon to pleat the wrapper up and around the filling.

5. Make a ring shape with your index finger and thumb. Pop the pleated dumpling into this circular cradle, then use the back of the spoon to press the filling firmly downwards so that it fills up all the nooks and crannies in the folds. This will help the dumpling keep its shape as it steams. Gently squeeze the dumpling as if you are cinching it in at the waist. Finally, nudge the base of the dumpling to create a flat, stable base.

**Makes 20–24**

4 dried Chinese mushrooms
pinch granulated sugar
400g pork loin or shoulder or pork mince
200g raw prawns, peeled and chopped into sweetcorn-sized pieces
20–24 round siu mai wrappers or square wonton wrappers
3cm piece carrot, finely diced

**for the marinade**

4 tsp finely diced ginger
½ tsp salt
¼ tsp ground white pepper
¼ tsp granulated sugar
1 tbsp light soy sauce
4 tsp Shaoxing rice wine
4 tsp sesame oil
½ tsp bicarbonate of soda
1 tsp cornflour

**to serve (optional)**

2 tbsp light soy sauce
chilli oil, to taste

6   Pop a few pieces of carrot on top of each dumpling then steam in in a bamboo steamer (or steamer), in batches, over vigorously boiling water for 7–8 minutes per batch.

7   Stir the soy sauce and chilli oil together in a small bowl. Serve the *siu mai* as soon as they have finished steaming, dipping them into the soy sauce mixture if you wish.

Along with Steamed Pork Buns and Pork and Prawn Open Dumplings, these complete the 'Guangdong big three' – the famous dim sum trio. The delight in making your own *har gau* is that you get to see the metamorphosis of the opaque white wrapper into a beautiful translucent skin that encapsulates vibrant pink prawns in the shape of a *gau*, or claw. Keep in mind that *har gau* are their tastiest without a dipping sauce, letting the delicate flavour of the prawn really shine.

# prawn claw dumplings

1. Combine all the filling ingredients in a bowl, then cover and chill for at least 30 minutes.

2. Stir the wrapper ingredients in a bowl. Add 200ml boiling water and use a pair of chopsticks to stir vigorously in one direction (e.g. clockwise). Use your hands to lightly knead and fold the dough until there are no lumps. Cover and leave the dough to rest for 5 minutes.

3. Roll the dough into a sausage and cut it into 24 pieces. Work with one piece of dough at a time, keeping the rest of the dough covered to prevent it drying out. Shape a piece of dough into a ball, then use a rolling pin to roll it out into a round wrapper about 8cm in diameter with a slightly thicker centre and thinner edges.

4. Pop a heaped teaspoon of the prawn filling in the middle, then fold the wrapper over into a semicircle. Cradle the wrapper in one hand, and use the other hand to create pleats along the edge furthest away from you, pinching the two edges firmly together after each fold to create a crescent shape. Aim for 7–8 pleats and start off with an extra wide pleat – this will help the dumpling to curve into a crescent shape. (For more dumpling pleating guidelines, see page 33.)

5. In a bamboo steamer (or steamer), steam the *har gau* in batches over vigorously boiling water for 7 minutes and serve immediately.

Makes 24
**for the filling**
*300g raw king prawns, peeled and roughly chopped*
*2 tsp finely diced ginger*
*4 tbsp finely diced canned bamboo shoots*
*½ tsp salt*
*2 pinches granulated sugar*
*2 pinches ground white pepper*
*1½ tsp cornflour*
*2 tsp sesame oil*

**for the wrappers**
*120g wheat starch*
*50g tapioca flour*
*2 pinches salt*
*2 tsp vegetable oil*

We think congee is magical because each grain of rice, suspended in an opaque pool of liquid, is like a velvety cloud that melts on the tongue. While fantastic as an unadorned base, plain congee can be jazzed up with toppings from the very traditional (century eggs) to the stuff of our childhoods (crushed chicken crisps). Just avoid soy sauce as this will make the congee taste sour and go watery. You'll need to soak the rice the night before for guaranteed fluffy grains.

# silken congee

1   Put the rice into a large bowl with plenty of cold water. Wash the rice by swishing it with one hand, then drain away the cloudy water. It may help to cup one hand under the stream of water to catch any escapees as you do this. Repeat until the water runs clear. Cover the rice with cold water and leave to soak overnight.

2   The next day, put the pork bones into a large saucepan, pour in enough boiling water to cover and leave for 2 minutes. Drain and discard the water.

3   Drain the soaked rice and add to the saucepan, together with the oil, salt and 1.5 litres water. If using, tear the *kong yu chu* into small shreds and add to the saucepan. Bring to the boil then cover, reduce the heat and simmer gently, stirring occasionally for 45 minutes, or until each grain of rice has burst open.

4   Gently stir 200ml boiling water into the pan to loosen the texture of the rice so that each grain is suspended in its own pool of congee. Serve with your toppings of choice, including *ja choi* if using, scattered over the top.

**Serves 4**
*100g jasmine rice*
*200g pork bones or 150g lean pork in one piece*
*½ tbsp vegetable oil*
*½ tsp salt*

**optional toppings**
*ground white pepper*
*sesame oil*
*toasted sesame seeds*
*sliced spring onions*
*boiled eggs, diced*
*century eggs, quartered into wedges*
*Chinese fried breadsticks*

 **add an exotic (see page 14)**
*1 piece of* kong yu chu *(dried scallops)*
ja choi *(preserved mustard stems), as a topping*

These golden batons hardly need an introduction. Gone are the days when spring rolls were largely eaten during the Spring Festival (aka Chinese New Year and hence the name 'spring' roll), for these little beauties are now adored all over the world – a ubiquitous finger food served at weddings, corporate functions and children's parties alike. Follow our frying tips below for super-crispy spring rolls.

# golden spring rolls

1  Soak the Chinese mushrooms for the filling in a bowl of hot water with a pinch of sugar for 30 minutes, then drain. Remove and discard the stalks and finely julienne the caps. If you are adding an exotic: soak the *mook yee* in hot water for the same length of time, then drain and finely julienne.

2  In a bowl, mix the pork mince, salt, sugar, pepper, ginger, garlic, ¾ teaspoon five-spice powder and 1 tablespoon water together, then cover and chill for 20 minutes.

3  Put the carrots and 2 tablespoons water into a saucepan and place over a medium heat. Cover and cook for a few minutes until the water has evaporated, then add the cabbage, mushrooms, *mook yee* (if using) and 100ml cold water. Reduce the heat to low and cook, uncovered, until the water has evaporated and the vegetables are tender. Transfer to a bowl and set aside.

4  Heat the vegetable oil in a frying pan over a medium heat. Add the pork and fry for a few minutes until browned. Reduce the heat to low, stir in the cooked vegetables, oyster sauce, sesame oil and remaining ¼ teaspoon five-spice powder and cook for 1 minute. Transfer to a bowl and leave to cool.

5  To make the spring rolls, wet a piece of kitchen paper and keep it nearby. Put one pastry sheet on a work surface with one of the corners pointing towards you. Put 2 tablespoons of the filling just below the centre, shape it into a sausage about 15cm long, then line up the top edge of the sausage with the side corners of the pastry. Fold the bottom corner of the pastry over the filling and tuck

## Makes 8–10

*8–10 sheets thin spring roll pastry*
*vegetable oil, for deep-frying*
*sweet chilli or Worcestershire sauce, to serve*

## for the filling

*2 dried Chinese mushrooms*
*½ tsp granulated sugar, plus extra for soaking*
*150g pork mince*
*½ tsp salt*
*pinch ground white pepper*
*1 tsp very finely diced ginger*
*1 clove garlic, finely diced*
*1 tsp five-spice powder*
*2 carrots (100g), halved and thinly julienned*
*100g white cabbage, shredded*
*2 tsp vegetable oil*
*1 tbsp oyster sauce*
*¼ tsp sesame oil*

**add an exotic (see page 14)**
*2g mook yee (cloud ear)*

it underneath the sausage, then make one full roll upwards. Wet the side flaps with the damp kitchen paper and fold them in towards the centre so that the newly folded edges are perpendicular to the bottom edge. It should now resemble an envelope. Wet the sides and triangular flap of the envelope (edges only) then roll the sausage upwards until completely sealed. Repeat.

6   Fill a large saucepan or a wok two-thirds with vegetable oil and place over a medium-high heat. For deep-fryers, set the temperature to 180°C/350°F. To test that the oil is ready, drop in a small piece of pastry; it should fizzle. Deep-fry the spring rolls for 1½–2 minutes, turning occasionally, until they are golden brown. Remove and drain on kitchen paper. Serve with sweet chilli or Worcestershire sauce.

*Guotie*, the traditional Chinese phrase for pan-fried dumplings, literally translates to 'pot stick', hence the popular name for these dumplings. The combination of a lush, juicy pork filling and crispy golden bottoms is so divine that stopping at one is impossible.

# pork potstickers

1  Using a pair of chopsticks or a fork, mix the flour, salt and 200ml boiling water together in a large bowl until you have a rough ball. Be careful, as the dough will be scorching hot. Remove it from the bowl and knead for 10 minutes, or until smooth.

2  Divide the dough into two even pieces, then use your thumbs to make a hole in the middle of each piece before stretching them out into bagel shapes with even thickness all the way round. Cover the 'bagels' with cling film and leave to rest for 20 minutes.

3  If you are using pork shoulder, cut roughly into 1cm cubes. Then use a heavy knife or a cleaver to *dhuk* (repeatedly chop) through the pork until it resembles coarse mince. Put the pork into a large bowl. Add the bicarbonate of soda, cornflour, seasonings, rice wine, soy sauces, sesame oil and 3 tablespoons water, then use a pair of chopsticks to vigorously stir in one direction (e.g. clockwise) until all the liquid is absorbed and the pork begins to bind to itself. Mix in the pak choi, spring onions, ginger and garlic.

4  Lightly flour your work surface. Cut one of the rested 'bagels' in half so you have two sausages the same size, then roll the sausages quickly, so they are evenly thick along their entire length. Line the two sausages together lengthways and cut them in half in the middle to create four mini sausages. Now line the four sausages lengthways to form a roughly square shape and cut through them three times to form 16 small pieces of dough. Repeat with the other 'bagel'.

*(continues overleaf)*

**Makes 32**
*300g plain flour, plus extra for dusting*
*pinch salt*
*1 tbsp vegetable oil*

**for the filling**
*300g pork shoulder or pork mince*
*½ tsp bicarbonate of soda*
*1 tsp cornflour*
*1½ tsp salt*
*1 tsp granulated sugar*
*pinch ground white pepper*
*1 tbsp Shaoxing rice wine*
*1 tsp dark soy sauce*
*1 tsp light soy sauce*
*2 tbsp sesame oil*
*200g pak choi, finely chopped*
*2 spring onions, thinly sliced*
*2 tsp finely diced ginger*
*1 clove garlic, finely diced*

**for the dipping sauce**
*1 tsp sesame oil*
*2 tbsp light soy sauce*
*1 tsp chilli oil*

5    Lightly toss the dough pieces in flour, then put a piece on the work surface, cut-side down, and flatten it. Roll the dough into a thin disc, about 9cm in diameter, then repeat with the remaining pieces. Keep the dough covered to prevent it drying out. If you are short on time, you could roll the dough to about 2mm thick and use a 9cm round cookie cutter.

6    To wrap the dumplings, put a heaped teaspoon of the filling into the centre of each wrapper. Fold over into a half-moon shape. Cradle the wrapper in one hand and use the other hand to create pleats along the edge furthest away from you, pinching the two edges together after each pleat as you go, to create a crescent shape. Avoid getting any filling on the edges and be sure to pinch firmly as you pleat to create a good seal.

7    Heat the oil in a large non-stick frying pan over a medium heat. Fry the dumplings, in two batches, flat-side down for about 2 minutes until a golden crust forms on the bottom. Add 100ml cold water and immediately cover with a lid (or a heavy plate). Let the steam cook the dumplings for 8 minutes, or until all the water has evaporated, then uncover and cook the dumplings for a further minute, or until they lift off easily from the base of the pan. Repeat with the second batch.

8    Meanwhile, mix all the dipping sauce ingredients together in a bowl. Tumble the dumplings onto a plate, making sure to show off their golden bottoms, and serve with the dipping sauce.

Just like a sigh-worthy baked potato, pan-fried *lo bak guo* (turnip cake) is soft and moreishly savoury on the inside with a perfectly thin and crispy skin on the outside. Although this dim sum is typically called 'turnip cake' on menus, it is actually made from a super-flavoursome snowy white batter of grated Chinese white radish and soaked rice flour.

# pan-fried turnip cake

1 Put the rice flour into a large bowl, pour over 150ml cold water to cover the flour completely, then cover and soak overnight.

2 The next day, soak the Chinese mushrooms in a bowl of hot water with a pinch of sugar for 30 minutes, then drain. Remove and discard the stalks then finely chop the caps. If you are adding an exotic, soak the *har mey* in a bowl of hot water for at least 20 minutes, then drain.

3 Lightly oil a 20cm loaf tin and set aside. Peel and grate the radish before putting it into a pan. If you have a really juicy radish, catch the juice and add it to the pan. Stir in the sugar, salt and garlic, then put the pan over a medium-low heat, cover and cook gently for 40 minutes, stirring occasionally, until the radish is soft enough to cut through easily with a plastic spatula. Drain the excess cooking juices into a measuring jug and set aside. Stir the white pepper, 1½ tablespoons oil and the rice wine into the cooked radish.

4 Using a pair of chopsticks, gently stir the soaked rice flour until it is a smooth slurry then gradually stir it into the radish. Add the mushrooms, *har mey* and *larp cheong*, if using.

5 You will need 100–150ml liquid of the reserved radish juices, so top up with cold water if necessary. Begin stirring this liquid into the radish mixture, testing the consistency as you do so by dipping a chopstick into the mixture then letting a drop fall onto the back of your hand: the drop should look like cloudy water but it should retain its shape on your hand rather than spread out.

**Serves 4**

*125g rice flour*

*3 dried Chinese mushrooms*

*1 tbsp granulated sugar, plus extra for soaking*

*1½ tbsp vegetable oil, plus extra for oiling and frying*

*500g Chinese white radish or mooli*

*½ tbsp salt*

*2 cloves garlic, finely diced*

*¾ tsp ground white pepper*

*½ tbsp Shaoxing rice wine*

*hot chilli sauce, to serve*

 **add an exotic (see page 14)**

*1 tbsp har mey (dried shrimp)*

*1 larp cheong (Chinese sausage), diced*

6   Pour the radish batter into the prepared loaf tin. Cover and steam over vigorously boiling water for 25 minutes, or until a skewer inserted comes out clean. Leave the *lo bak guo* to cool completely before turning it out of the tin. Slice the loaf into 1cm-thick pieces.

7   Heat 1 tablespoon oil in a frying pan over a high heat. Add the slices and fry until both sides are golden brown and crisp. Serve with the spiciest chilli sauce you can get your hands on.

DUMPLING SISTERS TIP
When choosing Chinese radishes, scratch them on the surface with your fingernail: you should only be able to scrape off a single layer of 'skin' before you reach the inside of the radish. Avoid radishes that flake off in multiple layers. The radish should also feel heavy for its size, indicating juiciness.

The mystery of these soup dumplings or *xiao long bao* is akin to that of the ship in a bottle: just how is the flavoursome broth captured within? 'XLB' devotees know that these are best eaten by first nipping at the foot of the wrapper with your front teeth and gently drinking the warming soup, before biting into the pork filling. So how is it done? Picture glistening gems of delicate jellied stock that are gently mixed into a pork filling. The stock melts during steaming. Mystery solved. Start preparing your *xiao long bao* either the night before or well in advance on the day to make sure your jellied stock sets.

# shanghai soup dumplings

1   In a small bowl, soak the gelatine powder in 100ml cold water for 10 minutes.

2   Heat the stock over a medium-low heat. If needed, season to taste. When the stock is hot but not boiling, gradually stir in the gelatine. Leave the mixture to cool completely, then transfer it to a bowl and chill for at least 3 hours.

3   After the stock has been setting in the fridge for at least 2 hours you can make the rest of the filling. Put the pork, ¼ teaspoon salt, 3 tablespoons water and the remaining filling ingredients into a large bowl, then use a pair of chopsticks to vigorously stir in one direction (e.g. clockwise) until the filling is combined. Cover and chill for at least 30 minutes.

4   Make the dough. Mix the flour and salt together in a large bowl. Make a well, add 6 tablespoons boiling water, then use a pair of chopsticks to stir vigorously along the edge of the bowl in one direction until the mixture resembles rough crumbs. Add 2 tablespoons cold water and the oil and stir vigorously until you have a ball of dough. Turn the dough out onto a floured work surface and knead for 8–10 minutes, then throw the dough onto the work surface with force. Throw the dough 10 times, then knead it for a further minute. Wrap in cling film and leave to rest at room temperature for 30 minutes.

**Makes about 20**

**for the filling**

1½ tsp gelatine powder

190ml pork stock

180g pork mince

½ tbsp very finely diced ginger

1 clove garlic, very finely diced

1 spring onion, thinly sliced

1 tsp light soy sauce

1 tsp granulated sugar

2 pinches ground white pepper

1 tsp vegetable oil

¼ tsp bicarbonate of soda

½ tbsp cornflour

salt

**for the dough**

210g plain flour, plus extra for dusting

2 pinches salt

2 tsp vegetable oil, plus extra for oiling

*(continues overleaf)*

5   When the stock has set and the pork has marinated, turn the jellied stock out onto a board. Roughly chop into cubes and add them to the pork mixture. Stir gently until combined, breaking up the stock slightly as you do so. Cover and freeze for 30–40 minutes until icy.

6   To wrap the *xiao long bao*, roll the dough into a sausage and divide it into teeny 8g portions. Work with just a few pieces of dough at a time, leaving the rest of the dough covered. Lightly flour your hands and the work surface. Shape a piece of dough into a ball, then roll it out into a 8cm circle. It should be fairly thin and the outer edge should be slightly thinner than the centre.

7   Cup the wrapper in the fingers of one hand and put a heaped teaspoon of the semi-frozen filling in the centre. Use your index finger and the thumb of your other hand to make pleats all the way around the edge of the wrapper, pressing firmly after each pleat to create a firm seal. When you reach the last pleat, twist the wrapper slightly to close the gap and pinch firmly together to seal.

8   Steam the dumplings in batches. Lightly oil a steam-proof plate or line a bamboo steamer with non-stick paper. Arrange the dumplings onto the plate (or steamer), making sure to leave a bit of space between each one. Steam over vigorously boiling water for 6 minutes. Leave to rest for 1 minute before serving.

*Char siu bao* are very special to our family because we have been selling them at the market for over 10 years. While the recipe is continually being tweaked to get the fluffiest buns, some magic ingredients remain a constant: a special low-protein flour that gives a tender crumb and ammonium bicarbonate for superior raising power. Make the extra effort to find these ingredients at the Chinese supermarket or online and you will be rewarded with cottony soft buns to sink your teeth into. It's a good idea to make the filling and dough starter the day before you want to eat these glorious buns.

# steamed pork buns

1  Make the filling. Combine 90ml water, any leftover marinade and scrapings from the baking tray after cooking the Char Siu Pork and enough hoisin sauce to bring the volume to a total of 200ml. If you are only using hoisin sauce, add the dark soy sauce and honey as well. Whisk in the flours until no lumps are visible, then pour the mixture into a small saucepan and stir over a medium heat until the sauce is dark, thick and glossy. Leave to cool, then mix in the pork.

2  For the starter, combine 60ml boiling and 120ml cold waters in a medium bowl and whisk in the yeast. Leave to activate for 10–15 minutes until frothy. In a large bowl, combine the flour and sugar, then stir in the yeast mixture to form a rough dough. Scrape onto a work surface and knead for a few minutes until smooth. Return to the bowl, cover with cling film and leave to rest in a warm place overnight for 8–10 hours or until it has almost tripled in size. It will be incredibly frothy.

3  The next day, make the dough. Dissolve the ammonium bicarbonate in 40ml water in a small bowl. Pour into the starter and use one hand to squelch the liquid into the dough until evenly combined. Add the flour, baking powder and sugar and stir to roughly combine. Turn out onto a work surface and knead for 5 minutes until the dough comes together. Don't worry if it feels slightly dry. Flatten the dough out slightly and spread on the lard. Envelope the lard in the dough

**Makes 14**

**for the filling**
*200ml hoisin sauce*
*½ tsp dark soy sauce (optional)*
*1 tsp honey (optional)*
*1 tbsp cornflour*
*1 tbsp plain flour*
*180g Char Siu Pork (page 189), cut into 5mm cubes*

**for the dough starter**
*½ tsp active dried yeast*
*320g low-protein flour*
*1 tbsp granulated sugar*

**for the dough**
*¼ tsp ammonium bicarbonate*
*180g low-protein flour*
*17g baking powder*
*100g granulated sugar*
*15g lard*

by folding it in on itself and knead for 10 minutes, until the dough is smooth and all the sugar crystals have melted. Shape the dough into a rough ball, cover and leave to rest in a warm place for 20 minutes.

4   Divide the dough into 14 pieces (about 60g each). Cover with cling film or a tea towel to stop them drying out. Shape each piece of dough into a rough ball, then flatten into a thick disc and roll out into a 9cm round. Aim to make the centre slightly thicker than the edges so it can support the filling better. Cover each wrapper as you finish the rest.

5   To wrap the buns, put a heaped tablespoon of filling into the centre of a wrapper and firmly pinch seven or eight pleats into it until the bun is completely sealed. As you finish each bun, put it on a square of non-stick paper and put it inside the steamer, leaving at least 3cm between each bun, until the steamer is filled. Repeat with the other wrappers and remaining filling, then leave the buns to rest for 10 minutes before steaming.

6   Steam the buns over vigorously boiling water for 8 minutes: resist the urge to peek because the first few minutes are crucial for getting the buns to burst open. Serve immediately or keep the steamer lid on until ready to eat. The buns keep in the freezer for 4 weeks if they have been steamed first. Re-steam from frozen for 15 minutes.

DUMPLING SISTERS TIPS

*Make it more refined*
For even fluffier buns with a more delicate crumb, use two starters instead of the one. Make starter one by activating 2g active dried yeast in 25ml boiling water and 50ml cold water, and mixing into 125g low-protein flour. Knead as in the method above and leave to rest for 4 hours. Starter two is made from starter one: take 100g starter one and add 500g low-protein flour, 280ml cold water and 1 tablespoon granulated sugar. Knead and then allow to rest for 8–10 hours. Simply use 500g of starter two in the final dough, and the rest of the recipe remains the same.

*Make it with plain flour*
Replace the low-protein flour with 220g plain flour and 100g cornflour in starter one and 120g plain flour and 60g cornflour in starter two. When making the final dough, increase the water to 50ml.

*Make it faster*
Replace the active dried yeast in the starter with fast-action yeast, reduce the starter resting time to 1 hour and use 10g baking powder in the final dough.

*Charn bao* shares the same filling as the Steamed Pork Buns (page 40) but it hits a different sweet spot with its heavenly soft, springy bread. To make the butter-enriched dough as light as a cloud we use the *tang zhong* or water-roux method. This means adding a cooked mixture of flour and water that locks moisture into the bread dough. Try it, and we promise you will be hooked.

# baked pork buns

1   Make the water-roux by whisking the flour and water or milk together in a small saucepan. Place over a low heat and whisk for 3–8 minutes until the tines of a fork leave tracks for at least 10 seconds when dragged along the surface. Transfer to a bowl, lay cling film so that it is touching the surface of the roux and leave to cool.

2   For the dough, stir the flour, sugar, salt and yeast together in a large bowl. Sift in the milk powder, if using. Weigh out 100g water-roux in another bowl and whisk in the milk and beaten egg. Stir this wet mix into the dry ingredients until roughly combined and then turn out onto a lightly floured work surface. This is a very tacky dough so begin by developing the gluten. Gather the dough in your hands and lift it above your head, then slap the dough back on the surface. Do 20–30 slaps in succession, then knead by repeatedly stretching the dough away from you and folding it back. Alternate between slapping and kneading for 10 minutes until the dough is very smooth. If the dough is too tacky, add a light sprinkling of flour – no more than a tablespoon in total.

3   Stretch the dough out to a 2cm thickness and spread on the butter. Take each corner of the dough and fold it into the centre until the butter is enclosed. Use firm pressure from the heel of your hand to coax the butter into the dough. Alternate kneading and slapping for 20–25 minutes until it is voluminous and silken, and passes the windowpane test: rip off a ping-pong ball-sized piece of dough and stretch it out into a square. If you can stretch it thin enough that light shines through without it tearing, move on to the next step. Put the dough back in the bowl, cover and leave to rest in a warm place for 1–1½ hours until doubled in size.

**Makes 12**

**for the water-roux**
*25g strong bread flour*
*125ml water or full-fat milk*

**for the dough**
*350g strong bread flour, plus extra for dusting*
*80g granulated sugar*
*½ tsp salt*
*7g (1 sachet) fast-action dried yeast*
*10g skimmed milk powder (optional)*
*100g water-roux (see above)*
*110ml full-fat milk*
*1 large egg (about 56g), beaten*
*30g unsalted butter, softened at room temperature*

**to fill and finish**
*1 batch Char Siu Pork filling (page 40)*
*runny honey, for glazing*
*toasted sesame seeds, for sprinkling*

4   Line a baking sheet with non-stick paper. Quickly knead the dough then divide into 12 pieces of about 60g each. Roll each piece into a 9cm circle and put 1 tablespoon of the filling in the centre. Gather up the edges and pinch together to seal. With the gathered side face down, shape the buns into domes and place them onto the baking sheet, leaving a 4cm gap between each bun. Cover loosely with cling film then a tea towel and leave to rest in a warm place for 1–1½ hours or until doubled in size.

5   Meanwhile, preheat the oven to 180°C/350°F/Gas mark 4. Bake the buns for 8–10 minutes until golden. Brush with honey and sprinkle with sesame seeds. Best eaten warm.

Whenever we go to *yum cha* as a family we always order at least two bamboo steamers full of *jing pai gwut* – bite-sized pieces of juicy pork ribs seasoned with fermented black beans. If you are a chopstick novice you will have a lot of fun trying to pick them up because of the glossy sauce that coats each rib. But once you get the little nugget into your mouth you will experience the mark of an excellent *jing pai gwut*: meat that pops off the bone with just the slightest encouragement.

# steamed black bean ribs

1  Slice between each bone to divide the rack into individual ribs. Place a rib on its side on the chopping board and use a cleaver to carefully divide it into bite-sized pieces. This is best done by using the corner of the blade nearest to the handle to strike the rib bone, as this generates the greatest force. If you are not confident about keeping your fingers while doing this, ask your butcher to do it for you.

2  Put the ribs into a large bowl, cover with water and coax the blood out of the bones and meat by carefully massaging them with your hands. Refresh the water as needed until it is almost clear. Drain the ribs in a colander.

3  Tip the ribs back into the bowl and add the cornflour, salt, sugar, light soy sauce and oil. Use one hand to massage all the seasonings into the ribs and to evenly distribute them. Now massage in the garlic, ginger and fermented black beans.

4  Arrange the ribs on a steam-proof plate (or steamer) in a single layer and steam for 8 minutes until there is no pinkness left around the bones.

**Serves 2**

*250g rack of pork ribs*
*2 tsp cornflour*
*¼ tsp salt*
*½ tsp granulated sugar*
*¼ tsp light soy sauce*
*1 tsp vegetable oil*
*1½ cloves garlic, roughly diced*
*½ tsp finely diced ginger*
*½ tbsp fermented black beans, rinsed and drained*

These magical little parcels are lovingly wrapped and steamed in rehydrated lotus leaves, which subtly perfumes the sticky rice with a slightly floral fragrance. A filling of plump Chinese mushrooms, saucy chicken and savoury pork make these a delectable meal-in-one . . . but in our experience, one is never enough.

# steamed lotus leaf parcels

1 Wash the glutinous rice in several changes of water until the water runs clear, then soak in a large bowl of cold water overnight.

2 The next day, lightly oil a dish (a round cake tin works well). Drain the rice and put into the dish then mix in the oil and salt. Steam in a large covered saucepan of hot water set over a medium heat for 40 minutes, or until the grains are translucent and tender to the bite.

3 Meanwhile, soak the Chinese mushrooms in a bowl of hot water with the sugar for 30 minutes. Remove and discard the mushroom stalks and slice the caps in half.

4 Prepare the filling by combining the pork, garlic, light soy sauce, salt, white pepper and cornflour in a bowl. Cover and leave to marinate for 20 minutes.

5 Rinse the lotus leaves under cold running water. Use a pair of scissors to cut each leaf into quarters, then trim off an equilateral triangle from the pointed end of each quarter. Put the leaves and trimmings in a large tray and soak in lukewarm water for 15 minutes. (You might need to use a plate to weigh the leaves down to keep them submerged in the water.)

6 Heat the oil in a frying pan over a medium heat and fry the ginger until fragrant. Add the marinated pork and fry for a few minutes until browned, then add the bamboo shoots and rice wine and stir until the alcohol cooks off. Turn off the heat and stir in the hoisin and dark soy sauces and the sesame oil, then transfer to a bowl and leave to cool to room temperature.

**Makes 8**
*4 dried Chinese mushrooms*
*pinch granulated sugar*
*2 dried lotus leaves*
*soy sauce, to serve (optional)*

**for the rice**
*320g glutinous rice*
*1 tsp vegetable oil, plus extra for greasing*
*pinch salt*

**for the pork filling**
*150g pork mince*
*½ clove garlic, finely diced*
*¼ tsp light soy sauce*
*pinch salt*
*⅛ tsp ground white pepper*
*½ tsp cornflour*
*½ tbsp vegetable oil*
*½ tsp finely diced ginger*
*120g bamboo shoots, diced*
*½ tbsp Shaoxing rice wine*
*2 tbsp hoisin sauce*
*¼ tsp dark soy sauce*
*¼ tsp sesame oil*

*(continues overleaf)*

**7** In a bowl, combine the chicken, ginger, cornflour, sugar, light soy sauce, sesame oil and ½ teaspoon water.

**8** To assemble each parcel, place a lotus leaf with the greener side facing down onto the work surface and the trimmed edge closest to you so it looks like a fan from your angle. Put one of the trimmed triangles in the centre to reinforce the base of your parcel. Wet your hands (to prevent sticking) and put 2 tablespoons of rice on top of the triangle. Use your fingertips to ease the rice out into a rough 6 x 8cm rectangle. Spoon ½ tablespoon of the pork filling onto the rice base and spread it out to within 1cm of the edge. Arrange two of the chicken pieces on top, tuck a halved mushroom in between, followed by a slice of *larp cheong*, if using. Re-wet your hands and flatten another 2 tablespoons of rice in the palm of your hand, and place over the rice base like a loose lid.

**9** To wrap each parcel, fold the bottom trimmed edge over the rice, followed by both side wings towards the centre, and then roll the whole thing up and away from you so the rice is completely encased. Set aside and repeat.

**10** Steam the parcels, in batches if needed, over vigorously boiling water for 15 minutes. Unravel the parcels just before eating and drizzle over soy sauce, if wished.

DUMPLING SISTERS TIP
Double the recipe and freeze leftover parcels once they have cooled down from steaming. To reheat, steam from frozen or even easier, give the parcel a blitz in the microwave until the lotus leaf can be peeled off and then cover with cling film and microwave until heated through.

**for the chicken**
*150g skinless chicken thighs or drumsticks, sliced into 16 pieces*
*3 slices ginger, cut into matchsticks*
*¼ tsp cornflour*
*¼ tsp granulated sugar*
*¼ tsp light soy sauce*
*¼ tsp sesame oil*

 **add an exotic (see page 14)**
*1* larp cheong *(Chinese sausage), sliced*

We have always marvelled at these *wu gok*: a feathery light and golden lattice surrounding the *faa* ('melt in the mouth') and fluffy pastry made from taro and split peas, enveloping a saucy pork filling. We believed that *wu gok* was a dish reserved for talented dim sum chefs and not mere mortals like us! It was Dad who developed this wonderful recipe for homemade *wu gok* that we just had to include in the book. These little beauties are actually quite simple to make, although they do require patience and careful measurements.

# taro puffs

1   Drain the split peas then put them into a steam-proof dish together with the taro and 2 tablespoons cold water. Steam over vigorously boiling water for 40 minutes.

2   Meanwhile, prepare the filling. Drain the mushrooms, remove and discard the stalks and dice the caps. Combine the mushrooms and all the remaining filling ingredients, except the prawns, in a bowl. Cover and chill for 20 minutes.

3   In a small bowl, mix together the pastry seasoning ingredients. Set aside.

4   Roughly mash the split peas and taro with a fork until soft and fluffy. Turn out onto a work surface and flatten slightly. Sprinkle over the pastry seasoning ingredients. Use a dough scraper or a knife with a wide blade to scrape in underneath the mixture at a 45° angle, then lift up and fold the mixture over on top of itself. Use the heel of your other hand to gently press downwards and forwards, as if you are smearing it across the work surface. Repeat until the seasonings are distributed throughout the dough – it should take a good 7–8 folds. Set aside.

Makes 8–10

*vegetable oil, for deep-frying*

**for the pastry**

*50g dried yellow split peas, rinsed then soaked overnight in cold water*

*150g taro, fresh or defrosted, cut into 2cm cubes*

*60g wheat starch*

*75g lard, softened*

**for the filling**

*2 dried Chinese mushrooms, soaked in cold water overnight*

*150g pork mince*

*2 tsp very finely diced ginger*

*½ spring onion, sliced*

*¼ tsp bicarbonate of soda*

*pinch salt*

*2 pinches ground white pepper*

*¼ tsp granulated sugar*

*¼ tsp sesame oil*

*35g raw prawns, peeled and diced*

*(continues overleaf)*

**5** Put the wheat starch into a bowl. Pour in 35ml boiling water, then use a pair of chopsticks to vigorously stir in one direction (e.g. clockwise) until the mixture resembles large breadcrumbs. Turn the mixture out onto the work surface and knead quickly until a slightly crumbly dough forms.

**6** Flatten the seasoned taro dough to a 2cm thickness and the wheat starch dough to a 1cm thickness, then put the wheat starch dough on top of the taro dough. Use the folding method described in step 4 to combine the doughs. Keep folding until the doughs are just combined. It will be sticky to the touch. Flatten the dough to a 2cm thickness, then put the lard on top. Work quickly to fold the lard into the dough using the same method until a soft dough forms. Wrap in cling film and chill for 2 hours.

**7** Meanwhile, cook the filling. Heat 2 teaspoons vegetable oil in a large frying pan over a high heat. Add the pork mixture and fry for a few minutes, or until cooked through, then add the prawns and cook for a further 2 minutes until pink. Remove the pan from the heat and leave to cool for a few minutes.

**8** In a bowl, mix all the sauce ingredients with 50ml water then stir into the cooked filling. Return the frying pan to a medium heat and stir until the sauce is thick enough to bind the filling together. Set aside to cool.

**9** Fill a large saucepan two-thirds with vegetable oil and put it over a medium-high heat. If you are using a deep-fryer, set the temperature to 200°C/400°F. Working as quickly as possible, wrap and fry two puffs at a time. Roll the pastry into a sausage and cut it into 30g pieces. Form one piece into a ball, then press down to create a 7–8cm disc. Put 1 heaped teaspoon of filling into the centre of the disc, then fold the disc in half, pinching the edges to seal.

**10** To test that the oil is ready for deep-frying, drop in a small piece of dough. It should fizz furiously, but not brown for at least 5 seconds. Carefully lower the *wu gok* into the oil and deep-fry for 30 seconds. Use a slotted spoon to roll the dumplings, then deep-fry undisturbed for 3–4 minutes until you can see the latticed surface. Remove and leave to drain on a wire rack with a baking tray set underneath. For a classic Cantonese presentation, sit each puff within a cupcake case.

**for the pastry seasoning**
*2 pinches salt*
*½ tbsp granulated sugar*
*2 pinches five-spice powder*
*¼ tsp ground white pepper*
*2.5g ammonium bicarbonate (see page 264)*

**for the sauce**
*¾ tbsp cornflour*
*½ tsp light soy sauce*
*½ tsp dark soy sauce*

*Cong you bang* are a rich and flaky flatbread, often found at *yum cha* and street markets. They are absolutely divine on their own, dunked in Silken Congee (page 26), or even used as a wrap for stir-fried dishes, such as Fragrant Cumin and Coriander Beef (page 78). The best thing about these is that they put the humble spring onion in the limelight: when fried within the multiple folds of a salty dough, the finely sliced spring onions impart a fragrant and super-satisfying savoury flavour.

# spring onion pancakes

1   For the dough, combine the flour and salt in a large bowl. Stir in the oil along with 260ml warm water until a ball of dough forms. Turn the dough out onto a floured work surface and knead for 5–10 minutes until it is smooth. If the dough is very sticky, add a little flour as you are kneading, but keep in mind that it should be a little bit sticky. Cover and leave to rest for 20 minutes.

2   Shape the dough into a sausage and cut it into 8 even-sized pieces. Work with one piece of dough at a time, keeping the rest covered. Roll the dough out into a rough square about 1mm thick. Drizzle on ½ tablespoon vegetable oil and use your fingers to spread it out across the surface as evenly as possible. Sprinkle 3 pinches salt and 1½ tablespoons of the spring onions evenly on top.

3   To form the pancake, take the edge closest to you and roll the dough as if you are rolling up a thin Swiss roll, then hold one end and roll it up again to form a snail shell spiral. Tuck the end underneath the spiral. Repeat with the remaining dough, cover and leave to rest for at least 10 minutes.

4   For each pancake, heat ½ teaspoon oil in a large frying pan over a low heat. Roll each pancake out into a circle. If you prefer a crispy pancake, roll it out to a 0.5cm thickness, and for a slightly chewier texture, roll the pancake out to a 1cm thickness. Fry for about 4–5 minutes on each side until golden brown and crispy, being sure to let all the layers cook through. Remove from the pan and fry the remaining pancakes.

**Makes 8**

*vegetable oil, for frying*

**for the dough**

*460g plain flour, plus extra for dusting*
*1 tsp salt*
*1 tbsp vegetable oil*

**for the filling**

*4 tbsp vegetable oil*
*6 spring onions, very thinly sliced*
*salt*

chineasy

Our taste buds have a guilty secret. Every now and then, they slink into their local Imperial Dragon and emerge with (gasp!) a clandestine box of glossy chicken cashew nut. Let's be honest: a good Chinese takeaway can be irresistibly delicious, supremely comforting and perhaps most importantly of all – easy. But even though we have devoured (and sold) our fair share of takeaways, we still believe that nothing is quite as delectable as homemade.

This chapter is our cure for the takeaway munchies. Every dish is at the 'lick the bowl clean' end of the tastiness spectrum, yet they are all straightforward, balanced, and all-in-one dishes that can be served atop rice or noodles for a complete meal. Many can be prepared in one pot for the ultimate in fuss-free cooking.

For the most part, we have provided serving quantities for one or two because these are exactly the sorts of quick-fire meals that we like to whip up when we find ourselves dining alone. If you have a crowd to feed in a hurry, simply scale up the recipes and cook up more of the great white grain.

There isn't another dish that represents solid, dependable Chinese food better than this one. Cooked with plenty of fresh vegetables, Chicken Cashew Nut is one of those all-time favourites that friends sheepishly admit to ordering every time they have Chinese because they 'just know it'll be good'. But we reckon that you will never order out again after trying our super-easy and lush home-cooked version.

# chicken cashew nut

1  Put the chicken into a bowl, add the marinade ingredients and ½ tablespoon water and stir well. Cover and chill for at least 20 minutes.

2  Heat 1½ tablespoons of the oil in a small saucepan over a medium heat. When a cashew dropped into the oil sizzles but does not brown, add the remaining nuts and shallow-fry for a few minutes until golden brown. Remove and drain on kitchen paper.

3  Put all the sauce ingredients in a small bowl, add 1½ tablespoons water, then stir well and set aside.

4  Heat ½ tablespoon of the oil in a wok over a high heat and stir-fry the ginger until fragrant. Add the mushrooms and 1 tablespoon water and stir-fry until all the water has evaporated. Add the peppers, onion and a further tablespoon of water, then reduce the heat to medium and stir-fry until the water has evaporated. Scoop the vegetables out of the wok and set aside.

5  Wipe the wok with kitchen paper and place over a high heat. Add the remaining ½ tablespoon of oil and stir-fry the chicken, stopping occasionally for a few seconds to spread the chicken out in a single layer on the base of the wok until the chicken is white, slightly singed and bouncy. Return the vegetables to the wok and stir-fry for 30 seconds.

6  Reduce the heat to medium, stir in the sauce and three-quarters of the cashew nuts and stir-fry for 1 minute to warm the sauce through. Serve with steamed rice, sprinkling the remaining cashews on top.

**Serves 2**

*200g skinless, boneless chicken breast, cut into bite-sized cubes*
*2½ tbsp vegetable oil*
*½ tbsp finely diced ginger*
*4 button mushrooms, halved*
*¼ green pepper, ¼ red pepper and ¼ yellow pepper, deseeded and chopped (or just one colour, if you prefer)*
*½ onion, roughly chopped*
*80g cashew nuts*
*steamed jasmine rice, to serve*

**for the marinade**
*½ tsp bicarbonate of soda*
*¾ tsp cornflour*
*2 pinches salt*
*¼ tsp light soy sauce*
*½ tbsp Shaoxing rice wine*

**for the sauce**
*1½ tbsp oyster sauce*
*½ tsp Shaoxing rice wine*
*pinch salt*
*3 pinches ground white pepper*

This dish was one of the very first dinners that Mum taught us to make when we moved away for university. The core combination of silky chicken, fragrant mushrooms and crunchy pak choi is fantastic, but it's also easy to add whatever else you like to the mix. Save on washing up by eating this one straight out of the pot, just like a real student!

# one-pot chicken rice

**1** Soak the mushrooms in a bowl of hot water with the sugar for 30 minutes, then drain. Remove and discard the stalks and chop the caps into a fine dice. If you are adding the exotics: cut off the hard nibs at the ends of the *gum choi* before soaking these and the *har mey* in hot water for at least 20 minutes.

**2** Put the chicken in a bowl, add the marinade ingredients and 1 tablespoon water and mix well. Cover and set aside.

**3** Put the rice into a small saucepan and rinse it twice under cold water, discarding the cloudy water each time. Pour in 80ml boiling water and bring to the boil over a high heat. Cook the rice for 4–5 minutes or until most of the water has evaporated, and there are small craters on the surface. Reduce the heat to the lowest setting.

**4** Add the mushrooms, softened *gum choi* and *har mey*, if using, to the marinated chicken and stir to combine, then arrange the chicken on top of the rice in a single layer. Crumble the *harm yu*, if using, into small pieces and nestle among the chicken. Cover and continue to cook for 4–5 minutes.

**5** Sprinkle the chopped pak choi directly on top of the chicken, cover and cook until the pak choi has softened slightly. Remove from the heat and leave the rice to stand for 3 minutes before drizzling soy sauce on top and digging in.

Serves 1

2 dried Chinese mushrooms
pinch granulated sugar
1 skinless, boneless chicken breast, cut into thin slivers
75g jasmine rice
60g pak choi or choi sum, sliced
light soy sauce, to serve

for the marinade
¼ tsp bicarbonate of soda
1 tsp cornflour
2 pinches salt
2 pinches granulated sugar
2 pinches ground white pepper
¼ tsp sesame oil
½ tsp light soy sauce
½ tsp finely diced ginger

 **add an exotic (see page 14)**
20g gum choi (golden needle vegetable)
10g har mey (dried shrimp)
10g chunk of harm yu (salted fish)

This one-pot wonder rivals the simplest weeknight stir-fry with its soy-seeped chicken, melt-in-the-mouth aubergine and sticky sauce. The key process is the transformation of a thin soy sauce mixture into a sweet and savoury syrup as it reduces down during cooking.

# syrupy soy chicken

1   Put the sauce ingredients into a bowl, pour in 250ml water and mix well. Set aside.

2   Heat the oil in a large frying pan over a medium heat and fry the ginger for 1 minute until it starts to blister and turn golden along the edges. Add the chicken in a single layer and brown for 2 minutes on each side.

3   Pour a third of the sauce mixture over the chicken: it will bubble furiously. Allow the liquid to reduce by a half. Turn the chicken over, add another third of the sauce mixture and reduce by a half.

4   Tuck the aubergine in between the chicken and pour over the remaining sauce mixture. When the liquid has reduced down to a light syrup and the aubergine is tender, toss the spring onions through until wilted. Serve the chicken, aubergine and sticky sauce with steamed rice.

Serves 4

1 tbsp vegetable oil
1 tbsp finely diced ginger
450g skinless, boneless chicken thighs, trimmed of fat
1 large aubergine (about 300g), cut into rough chunks
4 spring onions, cut into thirds lengthways
steamed jasmine rice, to serve

for the sauce
3 tbsp light soy sauce
½ tsp dark soy sauce
3 tbsp Shaoxing rice wine
2 tsp granulated sugar
1 tsp ground white pepper

If you only ever set out to master one truly superb Chinese dish, let it be a big steaming bowl of perfectly cooked egg fried rice. Filling, moreish and utterly foolproof, this recipe easily pips the restaurant versions. Simple secrets make all the difference: use rice cooked the night before to prevent mushiness, add two rounds of egg and fresh spring onions for an extra touch of vitality.

# eggy fried rice

1   Wash the rice in a medium saucepan in several changes of water until the water almost runs clear. Pour in 350ml boiling water and bring to the boil. Cook uncovered, until the surface is dry and dotted with little craters. Reduce the heat to low, cover and cook for a further 10–15 minutes until all the water is absorbed. Fluff up the rice then leave to cool on a baking tray, cover and chill overnight.

2   The next day, if you are adding an exotic: in a wok or large frying pan with high sides, fry the diced *larp cheong* until the oils are released and the edges start to blister. Remove and set aside.

3   Beat 3 eggs in a bowl along with a pinch of salt and 1 teaspoon oil. Heat 1 tablespoon oil in the wok over a medium-high heat. Add the beaten eggs and scramble for 30 seconds until just set. Transfer to a plate and set aside.

4   Wipe the wok with kitchen paper and return it to a high heat with 2 tablespoons oil. Fry the ginger until fragrant and add the cooked rice. Use a spatula to spread out the rice and separate the grains. Reduce to a medium heat and stir-fry for a few minutes until the rice is heated through. Add ½ teaspoon salt, the white pepper, sugar and soy sauces and stir-fry for a further minute until the rice is evenly coated with the seasonings.

5   Make a well in the centre of the rice. Add the remaining tablespoon of oil to the well and crack in the remaining eggs. Quickly beat the eggs then mix them through the rice to coat the grains and stir-fry for 2 minutes until the egg is cooked. Add the scrambled eggs, most of the spring onions and the *larp cheong*, if using, and stir-fry for a further minute. The rice is ready when it has become golden yellow in colour. Sprinkle with the remaining spring onions and serve.

**Serves 2**
*200g long-grain white rice (not easy-cook)*
*4 tbsp plus 1 tsp vegetable oil*
*5 eggs*
*1 tsp finely diced ginger*
*¼ tsp ground white pepper*
*1 tsp granulated sugar*
*1 tsp light soy sauce*
*¼ tsp dark soy sauce*
*2 spring onions, thinly sliced*
*salt*

 **add an exotic (see page 14)**
*1 larp cheong (Chinese sausage), diced*

These eggs are perfect when all you want is a light bite, just a little something to tide you over that is both filling and tasty. Give your taste buds an extra treat by cooking up some garlic and onion oil to fry the eggs in.

# garlicky broccoli eggs

**1** Steam or boil the broccoli until it is tender. Drain, then chop roughly until the broccoli is very small.

**2** Vigorously beat together the eggs, oil, salt and pepper until the eggs are frothy and well combined. Set aside.

**3** For the garlic and onion oil, heat the oil in a non-stick frying pan over a medium-low heat and fry the onion until soft. Reduce the heat to low, then add the garlic and fry for a 2–3 minutes until the oil is highly fragrant.

**4** Turn the heat up to high and add the chopped broccoli, then pour in the beaten egg. The egg should bubble up and cook rapidly. Scramble it, then plate up as soon as the eggs are partially set because they will continue to cook.

**Serves 1**
*150g broccoli, cut into florets*
*2 eggs*
*1 tsp vegetable oil*
*2 pinches salt*
*2 pinches ground white pepper*

**for the garlic and onion oil**
*1½ tbsp vegetable oil*
*¼ red onion, finely diced*
*2 cloves garlic, finely diced*

We hope this will become one of your go-to stir-fries as it is deliciously complex in flavour yet stunningly simple to make. Succulent nuggets of salmon swim among aromatic blades of garlic chives, while the final lick of dark soy sauce gives the whole dish a sense of luxury. Garlic chives are widely used in East Asian cooking and taste more like garlic than chives. Spring onions or baby leeks would also work well.

# salmon and garlic chives

1   Put the salmon in a bowl, add the marinade ingredients and ½ teaspoon water and mix to combine. Set aside.

2   Heat ½ tablespoon oil in a wok over a high heat and stir-fry the chives for 30 seconds until just softened, being careful not to let them char. Remove from the wok and set aside.

3   Reheat the wok and add the remaining oil. Add the salmon in a single layer and sear for 2 minutes until the pieces lift off the bottom of the wok without too much sticking. Stir-fry for a further 2 minutes until the pieces are slightly singed on all sides.

4   Return the chives to the wok, add the soy sauce, and toss until the sauce is evenly distributed. Serve with steamed rice.

**Serves 2**

*240g skinless salmon fillet, cut into cubes*
*1 tbsp vegetable oil*
*100g garlic chives, cut into 5cm lengths*
*½ tbsp dark soy sauce*
*steamed jasmine rice, to serve*

**for the marinade**
*¾ tsp finely diced ginger*
*¼ tsp granulated sugar*
*pinch salt*
*1 tsp cornflour*
*½ tsp light soy sauce*
*½ tsp vegetable oil*

There's something rather therapeutic about stuffing aubergine and peppers. Maybe it's the way you get to smooth over the top of the filling so they are neat, or maybe it's the anticipatory delight of fitting together the pieces of an edible jigsaw puzzle . . . whatever the joy is in making them, eating them is even better. From the silky aubergine and crisp peppers to the juicy pork filling, these are great with a liberal dousing of soy sauce.

# pork stuffed aubergine and rainbow peppers

1   Soak the Chinese mushrooms in a bowl of hot water with the sugar for 30 minutes, then drain. Remove and discard the stalks and dice the caps. Set aside.

2   Put the pork in a large bowl and add the marinade ingredients. Pour in 60ml water, then use a pair of chopsticks to vigorously stir in one direction (e.g. clockwise) until the meat starts binding to itself. Cover and chill for at least 20 minutes.

3   Slice the aubergines into discs about 3cm thick, then slice each aubergine disc, horizontally, three-quarters of the way so that the two layers of the aubergine are still attached by a 'hinge' and can open up like a puppet's mouth. Cut the peppers in half so you have little cups.

4   Add the chopped mushrooms and spring onion to the marinated meat, mix well, then use a butter knife to stuff the pork filling into the mouth of the aubergine discs and into the peppers. Smooth over.

5   Heat 1 tablespoon oil in large lidded frying pan over a high heat. Arrange the stuffed aubergine discs in a single layer in the pan. Fry for 1 minute before flipping them over. Add a further tablespoon of oil, tilting the pan to distribute the oil and fry for another minute. Pour in 60ml water and quickly cover. When all of the water has evaporated, reduce the heat to medium and fry for an extra minute before standing the discs up to brown the meat. Remove from the pan and cover with foil to keep warm. Heat 1 tablespoon oil and fry the peppers filling-side down for 2 minutes. Pour in 40ml water, cover and steam until all the water has evaporated. Serve the peppers and aubergines with a liberal drizzle of soy sauce.

**Serves 2**
*3 dried Chinese mushrooms*
*pinch granulated sugar*
*300g pork mince*
*2 large aubergines*
*¼ red pepper, ¼ green pepper and ¼ yellow pepper*
*¾ spring onion, thinly sliced*
*vegetable oil, for frying*
*light soy sauce, to serve*

**for the marinade**
*½ tsp salt*
*¼ tsp ground white pepper*
*1 tsp sesame oil*
*¼ tsp bicarbonate of soda*
*¾ tsp cornflour*
*2 tsp finely grated ginger*

Did you know that tofu also comes in a less wobbly, firmer variety? Firm tofu is fantastic for pan-frying because it injects some serious flavour and texture into this magical soy product. Just imagine sinking your teeth through a *cheow* (crunchy) seasoned crust to a delicate and *waat* (silky smooth) centre. Simply dress up your tofu steaks with a spicy soy sauce glaze and serve on rice for an easy and satisfying mid-week meal.

# pan-fried tofu steaks

**1**  Rub the pepper and chilli powder over the tofu.

**2**  Combine all the glaze ingredients, except the spring onion, in a small saucepan. Add 1 tablespoon water and cook over a medium heat for 3–5 minutes until it froths up vigorously. Remove from the heat and stir in the spring onion. As it cools the sauce will become a thick syrupy glaze.

**3**  Heat the oil in a large saucepan over a high heat. Working with one tofu steak at a time, pat the cornflour all over as densely as you can. The tofu steaks should be chalky white and dry to the touch. Add the steaks to the frying pan as soon as each one is coated. Fry the tofu for 2–3 minutes on each side until a crispy golden crust has formed. Arrange the steaks on a plate like a stack of fallen dominoes, drizzle with the glaze, sprinkle over the coriander and serve with freshly steamed rice.

**Serves 2**

pinch ground white pepper

pinch chilli powder, or to taste

300g medium-firm tofu, drained, sliced into thick steaks and patted dry

2 tbsp vegetable oil

3 tbsp cornflour

3 tbsp roughly chopped coriander leaves

steamed rice, to serve

**for the soy sauce glaze**

1½ tbsp light soy sauce

½ tsp dark soy sauce

3½ tsp granulated sugar

1 tsp Chinkiang vinegar, or ½ tsp balsamic vinegar

¼ fresh red chilli, thinly sliced or ¼ tsp dried chilli flakes

1 spring onion, whites only, thinly sliced on the diagonal

If there is one nugget of useful information we want you to absorb from this recipe, it is that cornflour can transform a quick vegetable stir-fry from 'it's good for you' to positively glitzy. Cantonese cooks often use a slurry of cornflour and water (*heen*) to finish their dishes because it adds gloss and luminosity. *Heen* is stirred through cooked ingredients over a low heat until it thickens. What you are aiming for is a transparent coating that is neither too thick nor too thin – one that will merely *gwa*, or just 'hang', off the ingredients.

# glossy vegetable stir-fry

1   If you are adding an exotic: soak the *mook yee* in a bowl of hot water for 30 minutes, then drain.

2   Fill a large saucepan with 1.5 litres water, add ½ teaspoon salt and bring to the boil. Blanch the baby corn first for about 1½ minutes, add the asparagus and broccoli and cook until all vegetables are slightly softened but still crisp. Drain in a colander.

3   Make the *heen*. In a bowl, mix the cornflour and 3 tablespoons water into a slurry and set aside.

4   Heat 1 tablespoon vegetable oil in a wok or frying pan over a high heat and stir-fry half of the garlic briefly to release its oils. Add the mushrooms and stir-fry for 2 minutes until plump. Add a pinch of pepper, stir-fry briefly then remove and set aside.

5   Add the remaining vegetable oil to the wok and put back on a high heat. Stir-fry the ginger and the remaining garlic until they release their aromas. Add the vegetables together with the drained *mook yee*, if using, and stir-fry for 2 minutes until each piece is lightly coated in oil.

6   Return the mushrooms to the wok, add ¼ teaspoon salt, a pinch of pepper, the sugar and soy sauce and stir to mix evenly. Reduce the heat, give the cornflour slurry a stir, then drizzle it into the wok. Use a fast stir-frying motion to move the vegetables around as the sauce thickens. Turn off the heat, add the sesame oil and serve.

Serves 2

65g baby corn, diagonally sliced

90g asparagus spears, diagonally sliced

200g broccoli, cut into chunky florets

1 tsp cornflour

2 tbsp vegetable oil

1 clove garlic, finely diced

100g oyster mushrooms, cleaned and torn into chopstickable pieces

1 tsp finely diced ginger

½ tsp granulated sugar

½ tsp light soy sauce

¼ tsp sesame oil

salt and ground white pepper

 **add an exotic (see page 14)**

4g mook yee *(wood ear mushrooms)*

If you are after a quick 'one-tray' supper that is packed with flavour, look no further than this recipe featuring *douchi*: fermented black beans with a distinctively sharp and salty flavour, and the magic ingredient in the 'black bean' stir-fries at the Chinese takeaway. Throw the *douchi* in with succulent beef strips, fiery chilli flakes, loads of garlic and a generous sprinkling of sugar before amping up the grill to caramelise the outside of the meat. Pop some fresh pak choi straight onto the tray for the final moments of cooking and voilà: dinner is served.

# black bean and chilli beef

**1** For the marinade, rinse the fermented black beans twice in cold water. Drain, then chop them roughly. Using the flat side of the knife blade, press firmly on two-thirds of the beans to mash them into a paste. In a large bowl, mix the black beans with the beef, the remaining marinade ingredients and 60ml water. Cover and chill for at least 30 minutes.

**2** Submerge the pak choi leaves in a bowl of cold water and set aside.

**3** Preheat the grill to high (250°C/480°F/Gas mark 9). Lightly grease a roasting tray with oil, then arrange the marinated beef in a single layer. Grill on the highest rack for 5 minutes, then flip the beef and grill for a further 2 minutes. Move the tray down to the middle rack and push the beef to one side. Fetch the pak choi, shake off any excess water and nestle it next to the beef. Season the pak choi with 2 pinches salt and grill for a further 1–2 minutes until it has just wilted and slightly singed. Sprinkle the coriander over the top and serve with steamed rice.

**Serves 4**

*400g beef rump steak, sliced against the grain into 5mm strips*
*400g pak choi, snapped off at the base*
*vegetable oil, for greasing*
*handful fresh coriander, roughly chopped*
*steamed jasmine rice, to serve*

**for the marinade**
*40g fermented black beans*
*4 cloves garlic, 2 roughly diced and 2 very finely diced*
*1½ tsp dried chilli flakes*
*1½ tbsp granulated sugar*
*½ tbsp Shaoxing rice wine*
*2 tbsp vegetable oil*
*½ tsp bicarbonate of soda*
*½ tbsp cornflour*
*salt*

We fondly remember discovering the combination of beef and cumin while we were on a childhood trip to Beijing. We had ordered grilled beef skewers from a little hole-in-the-wall shop, and we watched with anticipation as the shop owner lavishly showered on mysterious little brown seeds to encrust the beef entirely. As we dug in, the beef and toasted cumin pairing was the most marvellous explosion of flavour. Since then we have been hooked on cumin – and this is one of our favourite ways of cooking with it at home.

# fragrant cumin and coriander beef

**Serves 2**

*300g beef rump steak, sliced against the grain into 5mm strips*
*1 red pepper (about 220g), deseeded*
*handful fresh coriander, leaves and stalks separated*
*2 tbsp vegetable oil*
*½ medium onion (about 80g), sliced*
*1 tsp finely diced ginger*
*1 clove garlic, finely diced*
*1½ tsp ground cumin*
*½ tsp light soy sauce*
*steamed jasmine rice, to serve*

**for the marinade**
*1 tbsp cornflour*
*½ tsp light soy sauce*
*½ tsp dark soy sauce*
*¼ tsp salt*
*½ tsp bicarbonate of soda*
*½ tbsp vegetable oil*

1   Put the beef in a bowl, add the marinade ingredients and 2 teaspoons water. Mix well. Cover and chill for up to 4 hours (if you have time) or continue as below.

2   Cut the red pepper into eight segments then cut each segment into three diagonal pieces to create rhombus shapes. Dice the coriander stalks, then roughly chop the leaves and set both aside.

3   Heat 1 tablespoon oil in a wok over a high heat and stir-fry the onion briefly until it glistens. Add the red pepper and stir-fry until slightly softened and the onion is tinged with gold. Remove from the wok and set aside.

4   Add the remaining tablespoon of oil to the wok then briefly stir-fry the ginger and garlic. Arrange the beef in a single layer over the base of the wok and leave for 30 seconds, or until a slight crust has formed on the bottom of each slice, then stir-fry for 4 minutes until the beef has lost its pinkness. Add the cumin and coriander stalks and toss for 30 seconds until perfumed and fragrant.

5   Return the onion and red pepper to the wok together with the light soy sauce and toss to combine. Sprinkle in the coriander leaves, quickly toss again and serve with steamed rice.

sharing menu

At home we have always eaten dinner in the traditional Chinese family style where chopsticks shimmy across the table as everyone dips into the sharing dishes.

In the Cantonese tradition we usually start with a steaming bowl of soup (*tong*). As kids we would try to finish our soup as quickly as possible because the sharing dishes, or *sohng*, would already be tempting us with their aromas. *Sohng* literally means 'to accompany', for the rice (*fan*) is considered to be the most important part of the meal. Requests to *teem fan*, or 'add rice' to our bowls, was the sign of a healthy appetite. For our family of five it was normal to have three or four sharing dishes each night, which might have been a meat, fish, egg and veg plate.

To help you along, we have grouped the recipes in this chapter by the type of main ingredient. This way you can design a sharing meal using the same principles of nutritional balance as you would for any other type of cuisine, although here the serving sizes reflect a meal made up of several dishes.

We love this way of eating and the experience of a collective meal – the friendly debate over the tastiest plate of food, the bright colours on the table, the backing track of softly clicking chopsticks – is something we encourage you to explore.

When Mum starts counting down the days till we'll be home for the holidays, she always asks us what we'd like for dinner when we arrive. Without fail, at least one of us will enthusiastically request *shurn laat choi tong*: the Zhang family version of hot and sour soup is a cleansing broth chock-full with *leiu* (quality ingredients) including sriracha, a bright red and tangy chilli sauce that can be found in the international section at supermarkets.

# zhang fam's hot and sour soup

1   Using a pair of scissors, cut the vermicelli into 10cm long pieces, then soak in a bowl of cold water for 20 minutes.

2   Bring the chicken stock to the boil in a saucepan. Add the tomatoes and Chinese leaf or *harm shurn choi* and *ja choi*, if using, and return to the boil. Drain the vermicelli and add it, along with the mushrooms, chilli and chicken, to the saucepan and bring to a simmer. Stir in the salt and sugar.

3   Now work on creating a balance of hot and sour flavours by alternately adding white vinegar and sriracha sauce, tasting as you go until it's sharp, but also fiery. Serve in big bowlfuls.

**Serves 6**

*50g dried bean thread vermicelli*

*1.5 litres chicken stock*

*2 small tomatoes (about 80g each)*

*200g Chinese leaf, shredded (if not using the exotics below)*

*70g button mushrooms, sliced*

*1 medium fresh red chilli, deseeded and sliced*

*50g cooked chicken, shredded*

*½ tsp salt*

*1½ tsp granulated sugar*

*1¼ tbsp white vinegar*

*1½ tbsp sriracha sauce*

 **add an exotic (see page 14)**

*150g* harm shurn choi, *sliced (pickled mustard greens)*

*50g* ja choi, *sliced (preserved mustard stem)*

You will be hard pressed to find another recipe that is quite as quick, comforting, or foolproof as *dan fa* (literally, egg flower) soup. Perfect as a snack or as a light meal for one, the key is to pour the beaten egg in a thin stream at the very last minute to create silky strands that sit suspended in the soup. This soup is best eaten fresh because reheating will overcook the eggs.

# egg drop soup

1   Beat the eggs and egg white together in a bowl until frothy. In another bowl, mix the cornflour and 1 tablespoon water into a slurry and set aside.

2   Bring the chicken stock to the boil in a large saucepan over a medium heat. Just before the stock boils, gradually stir in the cornflour slurry, then stir in the bamboo shoots, ½ teaspoon salt, a pinch of pepper and the oil.

3   Reduce the heat to a simmer then gradually pour the beaten eggs in a thin stream, stirring, to form delicate ribbons. Season with more salt and pepper to taste, stir in the spring onion and serve immediately.

**Serves 2**

*2 eggs plus 1 egg white*
*2 tsp cornflour*
*500ml chicken stock*
*30g canned bamboo shoots, cut into slivers*
*1 tsp vegetable oil*
*½ spring onion, diagonally sliced*
*salt and ground white pepper*

Fans of coriander will love the fresh and cleansing flavour of this super-quick *gwun*-style (boiled) soup. It's the perfect light broth to serve before a sharing meal and it makes a great base for a light lunch, too. The very first meal that our little brother Justin learned to cook was coriander soup with thin egg noodles thrown in. It's still one of his favourite go-to meals today, so as long as Dad keeps a steady supply of coriander in the garden, Mum can rest assured that Justin will never go hungry.

# coriander and fish soup

1   Mix the fish, ginger, cornflour, oil and a pinch of salt together in a small bowl, then set aside. If you are adding an exotic, soak the *ji jook* in hot water for 20 minutes, then drain and finely slice.

2   Bring the chicken stock to a rolling boil in a saucepan. Add the coriander and *ji jook*, if using, and boil vigorously for 3 minutes. With the soup still boiling, stir in the fish and *gwun* (boil) for a further minute, stirring to loosen up the fish flakes.

3   Season the soup with the pepper, sugar and salt. Serve in bowls with cooked egg noodles if you wish.

DUMPLING SISTERS TIP
If you wish to add egg noodles, cook these separately in a pan of boiling water before adding them to the soup – this way the starch from the noodles won't make the soup gloopy.

**Serves 4**

230g white fish fillet, such as haddock or cod, thinly sliced

2 slices ginger, cut into matchsticks

2 tsp cornflour

1 tsp vegetable oil

1.2 litres chicken stock

140g fresh coriander

¼ tsp ground white pepper

½ tsp granulated sugar

1 tsp salt

240g egg noodles, see tip (optional)

 **add an exotic (see page 14)**

60g ji jook (dried bean curd)

Our earliest memory of watercress soup involves the somewhat clandestine harvesting of the watercress itself. The details are hazy, but as a young family we used to drive all the way to a relatively rural area of Christchurch to pluck huge bunches of wild watercress from a shallow stream. You can just imagine Dad's delight when he recently discovered there was watercress thriving near the stream where he and Mum go for their daily walks – now they can save the drive and have watercress soup whenever they like.

# watercress soup

1   Rinse the ribs thoroughly under cold running water, giving them a squeeze to coax the blood out of the bones.

2   Half-fill a large pan with hot water and bring to the boil. Add the ribs and boil rapidly for a few minutes. Discard the cloudy water, then pour in 2 litres hot water and bring to the boil. Add the carrots, ginger and dates. Return the stock to a rapid boil, then add the oil and watercress. Adding the oil with the watercress when the water is at its hottest will prevent the watercress from becoming *hai* (a rough mouthfeel) as it cooks.

3   Reduce the heat, cover and *boh* (cook on a rolling boil for a long period of time) the soup for at least 2½ hours.

4   When the soup is ready, season with salt to taste. We find that about ½ tablespoon salt works well for this volume. To serve, ladle the broth and a bit of everything else into each bowl. The meat should fall off the bones, and it is delicious dipped in light soy sauce.

**Serves 4**
*350g pork ribs*
*2 fat carrots, cut into large chunks*
*3 slices ginger*
*2 dried dates*
*1 tbsp vegetable oil*
*300g watercress (stalks and leaves)*
*salt*
*light soy sauce, to serve*

This popular soup is a permanent fixture on Chinese restaurant menus, but also surprisingly easy to rustle up at home. Juicy sweetcorn kernels, tasty morsels of chicken and delicate ribbons of egg make it the ultimate in comfort – a cheap and cheerful recipe that feels like a cosy blanket for the tastebuds.

# chicken and corn soup

1   Mix the chicken, soy sauce and a pinch of salt together in a small bowl, then cover and set aside. In another bowl, mix the cornflour and 100ml water into a slurry and set aside.

2   Put half of the sweetcorn and 250ml of the stock into a large pan, then use a hand-held stick blender to blitz the corn until it is a rough paste. Pour the remaining stock into the pan, then add the whole sweetcorn kernels and bring to the boil over a medium-high heat. Stir in the marinated chicken and cook the soup on a rolling boil for a further 4–5 minutes. Remove from the heat.

3   Give the cornflour slurry a quick stir, then gradually add it to the soup. Return the soup to a rolling boil and continue stirring for 1–2 minutes until thickened. Reduce the heat to a simmer and gradually stir in the beaten eggs to form wispy egg ribbons.

4   Season with ¾ teaspoon salt, the white pepper, and serve sprinkled with the sliced spring onion and sesame oil drizzled on top.

**Serves 4**

*1 large skinless, boneless chicken breast, chopped into small pieces*
*¼ tsp light soy sauce*
*3 tbsp cornflour*
*640g canned sweetcorn (drained weight)*
*1 litre chicken stock*
*3 large eggs, lightly beaten*
*¼ tsp ground white pepper*
*salt*

**to serve**
*½ spring onion, sliced*
*1 tsp sesame oil*

Each of the main ingredients in this soup – chicken, parsnip and ginger – work hard during a long, slow simmer to a create a milky broth that is definitely more spectacular than the sum of its parts. We hope that the first sip will take you by surprise as you detect notes of honey, the second sip make you wonder why you have never had it before, and the third sip have you planning the next batch.

# chicken and parsnip soup

1  Remove and discard the skin from the chicken drumsticks then rub them all over with salt. Put the drumsticks into a large pan and pour over boiling water, leave to sit for a few minutes to draw out the blood, then drain and discard the water.

2  Clean out the pan, add the oil and put over high heat. Add the ginger and fry for a minute, then brown the drumsticks in the fragrant oil for a few minutes. Pour in 120ml water then cover immediately and let it bubble furiously for 2 minutes.

3  Pour in 1.5 litres boiling water, add the parsnip, cover and simmer for a further 1½–2 hours. The soup is ready to season when the liquid has turned milky and the parsnips are starting to melt into the soup. Season with salt to taste and serve.

**Serves 4**

*4 chicken drumsticks (about 450g)*

*1 tbsp vegetable oil*

*1 thumb-sized piece ginger, peeled, halved and smashed*

*1 large parsnip (about 200g), cut into large chunks*

*salt*

The West Lake in Zhejiang Province in eastern China is an UNESCO World Heritage Site famed for its natural beauty and historic relics. It is said to have served as the muse for many poets and painters and, in the form of this soup, has even influenced the culinary arts. West Lake soup is simple to make and despite not using a stock or a long simmering time, this silky, fragrant soup is as tasty and gratifying as any others in this book. For the ultimate *waat* (silky) mouthfeel replace the cornflour with arrowroot powder.

# west lake soup

1 Soak the Chinese mushrooms in a bowl of hot water with the sugar for 30 minutes. Drain, remove and discard the stalks, thinly slice the caps, then set aside. In a small bowl, combine the beef and 1 teaspoon cornflour and set aside.

2 Bring 1.2 litres water to the boil in a large saucepan. Stir in the soy sauce, salt and pepper, then add the mushrooms and beef. Use a pair of tongs or chopstick to swizzle the water vigorously, breaking up any large lumps of meat. Partially cover, return to the boil, then reduce the heat and simmer for 10 minutes. Add the tofu and simmer for a few minutes until the tofu has heated through.

3 In a bowl, mix the 6 tablespoons cornflour and 100ml water into a slurry, then pour the slurry into the soup. Increase the heat to medium and stir continuously until the soup thickens.

4 Drizzle in the beaten egg whites, tracing a spiral path. Leave the eggs to set for about 15 seconds, then use a ladle to stir the egg through the soup until the egg is completely set.

5 Add the coriander, cook until it has just wilted, and serve.

**Serves 4**

*4 dried Chinese mushrooms*
*pinch granulated sugar*
*200g beef mince*
*1 tsp plus 6 tbsp cornflour or arrowroot powder*
*1 tbsp light soy sauce*
*½ tsp salt*
*¼ tsp ground white pepper*
*100g soft tofu, cut into cubes*
*3 egg whites, lightly beaten*
*large handful fresh coriander (about 30g), chopped*

These speedy 'dumplings' are as fun to make as they are to eat. On the outside they look like tiny omelettes, but take a bite and you will be greeted with an aromatic filling of pork and spring onion. These dumplings have a tendency to behave like a batch of pancakes in that the first one you make is likely to be misshapen, although we are sure you will love it just the same.

# half-moon egg dumplings

1   Put all the filling ingredients in a bowl, add 1 teaspoon water and stir in one direction (e.g. clockwise) until everything binds together. Leave to marinate for 15 minutes, if you have time.

2   In another bowl, whisk together the eggs with the oil, salt, pepper and spring onion.

3   Lightly oil a non-stick frying pan and place over a medium heat. Working as quickly as you can, spoon about a tablespoon of the egg mixture into the pan and use the back of your spoon to spread the pool out into a circle. Now put a teaspoon of the filling onto one half of the circle, leaving about 5mm of egg around the edge. Quickly fold the other half over the filling before the egg sets and press to seal the edges, flattening the filling slightly as you do so. Move on and set up another dumpling once the edges are sealed.

4   Fry each dumpling on both sides for a minute or so until golden all over. It's important to give the filling a chance to cook through; have a peek inside if you're unsure, and reduce the heat if the egg colours before the filling is cooked. Serve the dumplings with a drizzle of soy sauce.

Serves 4

for the filling

*150g pork mince*
*1 clove garlic, finely diced*
*1 spring onion, thinly sliced*
*1 tsp cornflour*
*large pinch bicarbonate of soda*
*1 tsp light soy sauce, plus extra to serve*
*large pinch ground white pepper*
*1 tsp sesame oil*
*large pinch salt*

for the eggs

*4 large eggs*
*½ tsp vegetable oil, plus extra for oiling*
*2 pinches salt*
*pinch ground white pepper*
*1 spring onion, very thinly sliced*

This Chinese version of an egg omelette is as smooth as velvet. The key is to nurse the oil into the eggs during cooking so some of it is absorbed while the rest is enveloped within the layers of ribbony egg. You can replace the prawns with garlic chives or simply make the eggs on their own.

# pillow eggs

1   Whisk the eggs with the salt, pepper, sugar and 2 tablespoons oil in a bowl. Add the prawns, if using.

2   Heat 1 tablespoon oil in a wok or a frying pan with high sides over a medium heat. Pour in the eggs and immediately use a spatula to swirl the egg in a languid circular motion. When you can see the egg starting to set, drizzle 2 tablespoons oil around the edge and let it seep into the egg as you keep swirling. When the oil has been absorbed, add another tablespoon of oil and resume the swirling. You are aiming to build wide ribbons of egg that interweave with each other.

3   Once the egg is about 80 per cent set (you will still see pools of egg trapped in the ribbons), stop swirling and cook for a minute until the egg just starts to colour on the bottom. Divide in half and flip each half to colour the other sides, then serve.

**Serves 4**
*5 large eggs*
*¼ tsp salt*
*large pinch ground white pepper*
*large pinch granulated sugar*
*90ml vegetable oil*
*100g raw king prawns, peeled*

The best part of this dish is its simplicity: a mixture of eggs and water that transforms into a tender and silky wonder via the magic of steam. An old rule of thumb is that every egg should have three half-eggshells worth of water added to it. You can replace the water with chicken stock for more flavour, and/or add spring onions, fish fillets, dried shrimp or dried scallops.

# silky steamed eggs

1   If you are adding an exotic: rinse the *kong yu chu* then soak in a bowl of cold water for 30 minutes. Use your fingers to break up the natural fibres then put in a small microwave-safe bowl. Add 2 teaspoons of the soaking liquid and set the remaining liquid aside. Rub in the cornflour and salt. Microwave, covered, for 30 seconds. Set aside.

2   Put the eggs, salt and sugar in a large bowl. Using a halved eggshell as a measure, add 12 measures of cold water (about 200ml) and whisk everything well. Pour the eggs into a steam-proof dish: if you want a mirror-smooth surface, pour the eggs through a sieve first to catch the froth. If using *kong yu chu*, use the soaking liquid along with any additional cold water needed to make up the 12 measures, and after transferring to the steaming dish, scatter in half of the *kong yu chu*.

3   Bring some water to the boil in a wok or large saucepan that will fit your dish, with a steaming rack set inside. Use a glass lid if you have one as it will help you see when the egg is ready. Add the eggs then reduce the heat to the lowest setting and steam for 6–8 minutes until the eggs are set but still wobbly in the centre. If you see them puffing up, briefly lift the lid to release some steam. Scatter over the remaining *kong yu chu*, if using, at the 4 minute mark and steam until set. Serve with a drizzle of light soy sauce and sesame oil along with a sprinkling of pepper.

**Serves 4**
*4 large eggs*
*¼ tsp salt*
*3 pinches granulated sugar*

**to serve**
*light soy sauce*
*sesame oil*
*ground white pepper*

 **add an exotic (see page 14)**
*3 kong yu chu (dried scallops)*
*¼ tsp cornflour*
*pinch salt*

It speaks a lot to the fame of this Sichuanese dish when it is regularly cooked to feed a Cantonese family, as it was in our house. While tofu is the main component, its true role is to carry the incredible cast of ingredients that it mingles with, especially the fiery and savoury chilli bean sauce and the flotilla of Sichuan pepper.

# mapo tofu

1   Steep the cubed tofu in lightly salted boiling water (about ¼ teaspoon salt per 500ml).

2   Meanwhile, mix ½ teaspoon cornflour into the beef. Heat 1 teaspoon oil in a wok or large frying pan over a high heat and briefly fry half the garlic and ginger until fragrant. Add the beef and brown, breaking up any large pieces as you go. Remove and set aside.

3   In a bowl, mix the remaining cornflour and 2 tablespoons water into a slurry and set aside. Carefully drain and discard the water from the tofu. Heat 3 tablespoons oil in the same frying pan, over a medium heat, and stir-fry the chilli bean sauce for a few minutes until the oil turns a deep red colour and you feel like you're standing inside a comforting cloud of spicy smells.

4   Stir in the remaining ginger and garlic, and beans, if using, then return the beef to the pan, slide in the tofu, and pour 125ml water on top. Gently slide your frying pan back and forth to encourage the tofu cubes to nestle together under the liquid. Bring to the boil, then reduce the heat and simmer for a few minutes as the tofu works on soaking up the flavours. Gently stir in a pinch of salt, pepper and the sugar.

5   Give the cornflour slurry a stir and drizzle it into the pan. Delicately stir the mixture as the sauce thickens and becomes glossy. Stir through the spring onion and serve sprinkled with ground Sichuan pepper.

DUMPLING SISTERS TIP
Make it vegetarian by omitting the beef or replace it with diced onions, mushrooms or aubergine. Just pre-cook as you would for the beef and follow the recipe as per above.

**Serves 4**

500g soft tofu, cut into 2cm cubes
2 tsp cornflour
100g beef mince
vegetable oil, for cooking
1 clove garlic, finely diced
1cm piece ginger, finely diced
2 tbsp chilli bean sauce
1 tbsp fermented black beans, roughly chopped (optional)
½ tsp granulated sugar
1 spring onion, thinly sliced diagonally
salt and ground white pepper
½ tsp ground Sichuan pepper, to serve

Growing up we often indulged in fresh New Zealand mussels sold at our local fish market. Most of the time, we would simply poach them and serve alongside a little soy sauce. Here is a special way to have them that sets the rich umami of *douchi* (fermented black beans) against the natural sweetness of the mussels.

# black bean steamed mussels

1  Rinse the mussels under cold water and brush off any dirt, if needed. Tap any open mussels and discard if they don't close. If you are right handed, hold each mussel with your left hand on its side with the flatter, more stable edge as the base. Slide the tip of a small knife in the slit where the shells meet and pry open. Use the knife to release the mussel meat from one half of the shell, slicing under the tough white tube of muscle stuck to the shell as you do so, then tear off and discard the meatless shell. Rinse the mussels under cold water and drain. Arrange each shell on a steam-proof plate so it forms a bowl for the cooking juices to collect in during steaming.

2  Rinse the fermented black beans under cold water. Chop them roughly, add the diced garlic, then use the side of a wide knife to crush the beans into a rough paste. Use the knife to fold in the sugar, cornflour and oil. You can do this in a small bowl with a spoon, if you prefer.

3  Pinch off black bean-sized nuggets of paste and place a few nuggets on top of each mussel. Steam the mussels for 3 minutes with the water at full boil. Eat the mussels straight from the shell, slurping up the fragrant juices as you do so.

**Serves 4**

*500g fresh mussels*

*2 tbsp fermented black beans*

*1½ cloves garlic, very finely diced*

*pinch granulated sugar*

*½ tsp cornflour*

*1 tsp vegetable oil*

In an excellent demonstration of 'keeping it simple', we think that one of the most perfect ways to preserve and savour the clean, sweet taste of prawns is by blanching them. On holiday in Venice we came across a seafood market that boasted giant piles of fresh prawns. That night we devoured the sweetest prawns that any of us had ever eaten. We simply blanched and ate them dipped into a slightly spicy, raw-garlic infused soy sauce. It was so sublime that our *ye jay do yook mai* (ears wiggled)!

# blanched prawns with garlic soy

1   Mix all the dipping sauce ingredients in a small bowl and set aside.

2   Pour 1.5 litres cold water into a medium saucepan, add 2 pinches of salt and put it over a high heat. Small bubbles will begin to appear on the base of the saucepan. The prawns are ready to go into the water when the bubbles have reached the *har arn sui* (literally, 'prawn eye water') stage. This is when the bubbles on the bottom of the saucepan have grown to the size of a prawn's beady eye, but before the water has started to boil. Add the prawns and bring the water to the boil. The prawns are ready to devour when they float to the top and are vibrant pink in colour. Drain and serve immediately with the garlicky dipping sauce.

**Serves 4**
*400g raw king prawns, shell-on*
*salt*

**for the dipping sauce**
*4 tsp light soy sauce*
*2 cloves garlic, very finely chopped*
*¾ tsp sesame oil*

We understand why some people are wary of cooking squid: you have to find some, clean them and hope it doesn't cook up as rubbery tubes. However, here in the UK, we have found that it is fairly easy to find bags of frozen cleaned squid tubes in fishmongers. To reduce the risk of rubberiness, simply use the bicarbonate of soda trick to relax the proteins in the squid meat before cooking.

# spicy squid stir-fry

1   Thoroughly rinse the squid tubes under cold water. Open up the tube by sliding a knife inside and slicing along one of the folded edges. With the inside facing up, use a very sharp knife to score the entire surface with parallel cuts. For the most impressive curling action, try to angle the blade of your knife at a 45° angle to the surface of the squid, score as deep as you can without going through to the other side, and keep the scores only a few millimeters apart. Rotate the piece of squid by 180°, and score again so that you end up with a cross-hatch pattern. Cut the scored squid into 4 x 4cm sized pieces, drain in a colander and mix in the bicarbonate of soda.

2   Separate the white part of the spring onion from the green and finely slice. Slice the green parts on the diagonal into long shards. Set aside.

3   Heat ½ tablespoon oil in a wok or frying pan over a high heat and stir-fry the onion until softened. Remove and set aside.

4   Reheat the wok or frying pan until smoking hot. Add 2 tablespoons oil, rapidly followed by the spring onion whites and ginger and stir-fry until fragrant. Add the chilli and stir a few times to tease the heat out of the chilli and into the oil.

5   Add the squid and stir-fry until they have all curled up into tubes. Add the hoisin sauce, pepper, salt and sugar and toss to mix everything together. Add the spring onion greens and stir-fry until they have wilted slightly, then serve.

**Serves 4**

*3 large squid tubes (about 450g in total)*
*2 pinches bicarbonate of soda*
*2 spring onions*
*2½ tbsp vegetable oil*
*1 medium onion, sliced*
*½ tbsp diced ginger*
*½ fresh red chilli, deseeded and diagonally sliced*
*2 tbsp hoisin sauce*
*¼ tsp ground white pepper*
*pinch salt*
*large pinch granulated sugar*

This way of preparing fish has the hallmarks of Cantonese cooking stamped all over it, where simple seasonings enhance the natural flavours of the freshest ingredients possible. Here, the fresh fish takes centre stage and is minimally adorned with ginger and spring onions and bathed in a pool of sweetened soy sauce. A final dramatic drizzle of smoking hot oil extracts flavour from the spring onion and ginger, which then mingles with the sauce.

# whole steamed fish

1  In a bowl, mix the cornflour and 1 teaspoon water into a slurry. Rub the salt all over the fish, followed by the cornflour slurry, then ½ teaspoon oil. Lightly oil a steam-proof plate and put the fish on top. Steam over a high heat for 10–12 minutes, periodically topping up the water if needed. You can check for doneness by inserting a chopstick into the fleshiest part of the fish along its backbone; the juices should run clear and the flesh should easily flake off the bone.

2  While the fish is steaming, dissolve the sugar in 3 tablespoons boiling water in a small bowl. Mix in both soy sauces and set aside.

3  When the fish is cooked, gently transfer it to a serving platter. Pour the soy sauce mixture on top and pile on the spring onion and ginger.

4  In a small saucepan, heat the remaining oil and the chilli, if using, until the oil just starts to smoke and pour evenly over the fish, and serve.

**Serves 4**

*½ tsp cornflour*

*¼ tsp salt*

*700g whole sea bass, scaled, gutted and cleaned, then patted dry*

*3 tbsp vegetable oil, plus extra for oiling*

*1 tsp granulated sugar*

*1 tsp dark soy sauce*

*2 tbsp light soy sauce*

*1 spring onion, thinly sliced diagonally*

*3cm piece ginger, cut into matchsticks*

*1 fresh red chilli, sliced (optional)*

These wings delight all five senses. They taste incredibly moreish, entice you with their cooking aroma, encourage you to tuck in with your fingers, look crispy before your teeth confirm that is the case and treat you to a cacophony of bubbling sounds as they crisp up in the oven. If you fancy yourself a bit of a chopstick pro then see if you can work the meat off with just teeth and chopsticks – stabbing is cheating!

# crispy five-spiced chicken wings

**Serves 4**

*500g chicken wings, tips removed, separated into drumettes and flats (see tip)*
*½ tbsp vegetable oil*
*¼ tbsp salt*
*1 tsp five-spice powder*

1   Preheat the oven to 200°C/400°F/Gas mark 6. Line a baking sheet with foil and set a wire rack on top. Toss the chicken in the oil and salt, making sure to evenly distribute the salt over the surface of the skin. Spread the chicken out onto the rack, making sure that they don't touch.

2   Bake for 45–50 minutes until cooked through and crispy, turning halfway through.

3   Immediately transfer to a large bowl and sprinkle over the five-spice powder. Toss to coat evenly. The skins will crisp up further as the wings cool.

DUMPLING SISTERS TIP
The 'drumette' is the first section of the chicken wing between the shoulder and elbow while the 'flat' is the section between the elbow and the tip.

There's nothing quite like the inviting, nutty aroma and crunch of toasted sesame seeds. In this recipe they co-star with a richly flavoured poached chicken to deliver a quick and satisfying dish. If you find yourself with leftovers, the chicken and sauce is excellent wedged into a crusty baguette with salad leaves.

# sesame-flecked chicken

1   Heat the vegetable oil in a medium saucepan over a medium-high heat and fry the ginger and spring onions until the ginger starts to blister. Quickly stir in the salt, pour in 250ml hot water and immediately cover with a tight-fitting lid. Let the mixture boil vigorously for 2 minutes to extract flavour from the aromatics.

2   Add both soy sauces, rice wine, pepper, sugar, ½ teaspoon sesame oil and the chicken to the saucepan. Cover, bring to a gentle simmer and poach the chicken for 15 minutes, turning halfway through. Remove the chicken from the pan and set aside. With the lid off, bring the liquid in the saucepan to the boil and reduce the volume to half.

3   Meanwhile, toast the sesame seeds in a small frying pan over a low heat for 2–5 minutes, or until golden and fragrant, swirling occasionally to prevent burning.

4   To serve, roughly shred the chicken using your hands or two forks and arrange in a shallow dish. Pour the reduced sauce over the shredded chicken, drizzle over the remaining 1 teaspoon sesame oil and sprinkle with the sesame seeds, letting some of them float on the moat of sauce around the chicken.

**Serves 4**

½ tbsp vegetable oil

6 slices ginger, cut into fine matchsticks

3 spring onions, white parts only, thinly sliced diagonally

¼ tsp salt

1 tbsp light soy sauce

¼ tsp dark soy sauce

½ tbsp Shaoxing rice wine

¼ tsp ground white pepper

½ tbsp granulated sugar

1½ tsp sesame oil

600g skinless, boneless chicken thigh fillets

1½ tbsp sesame seeds

This recipe is for a truly classic home-style dish that has survived the Chinese diaspora to reach all corners of the globe. Its enduring appeal is easy to understand: the chicken is beautifully tender, everything is mixed then steamed in the one dish, and it is self-saucing, making it the perfect partner for steamed rice.

# fragrant steamed chicken

1   Soak the Chinese mushrooms in a bowl of hot water with the sugar for 30 minutes, then drain. Remove and discard the stalks and cut each cap into three strips. If adding an exotic: pinch off and discard the hard end of the *gum choi*, soak in a bowl of hot water for 30 minutes then drain. Soak the *mook yee* in a separate bowl of hot water for 30 minutes, then drain.

2   Combine all the ingredients in a steam-proof dish, including the mushrooms and drained *gum choi* and *mook yee*, if using, along with 1 tablespoon water. Cover and chill for at least 20 minutes.

3   Steam for 10 minutes over a vigorous boil, then serve.

**Serves 4**

*4 dried Chinese mushrooms*
*pinch granulated sugar*
*300g skinless, boneless chicken thighs, cut into 3cm strips*
*2 slices ginger, cut into very fine matchsticks*
*1 tsp cornflour*
*¼ tsp salt*
*¼ tsp granulated sugar*
*large pinch ground white pepper*
*¾ tsp light soy sauce*
*1½ tsp vegetable oil*
*1 tsp sesame oil*

**add an exotic (see page 14)**

*10g* gum choi *(golden needle vegetable)*
*5g* mook yee *(wood ear mushrooms)*

Curry doesn't usually spring to mind when one thinks of Chinese food but we have happy memories of eating this. The potatoes are cooked until they are just falling apart and have guzzled up the coconut, curry and chicken flavours. The result is an incredible *faa* mouthfeel – crumbly and melty. Then there is the sauce. Perfect for *paa fan*, just hold the rim of the rice bowl against your lower lip and shuffle everything into your mouth with chopsticks.

# potato and chicken curry

1  Rub a few pinches of salt over the chicken pieces. Heat 1 tablespoon oil in a saucepan over a medium heat and stir-fry the ginger until fragrant. Add the chicken and brown well on both sides, being sure to render the fat out of the skin, then remove and set aside.

2  Heat the pan again and add the remaining tablespoon of oil. Fry the curry powder until it darkens and the air is perfumed with curry smells. Tip in the potatoes and stir-fry for about a minute until the curry powder latches onto the surface of each cube of potato. Pour in the coconut milk (reserving about a tablespoon), stock or water, sugar and ¼ teaspoon salt and gently mix to combine. Cover and simmer over a medium-low heat for 12 minutes, stirring occasionally until the potatoes have softened slightly.

3  Return the chicken to the pan, nudging each piece between the potatoes and making sure that they are covered in the sauce. Cover and simmer for a further 10 minutes until the chicken and potatoes are cooked through and the potato cubes have lost their sharp edges.

4  Turn off the heat and mix in three-quarters of the chopped coriander. Serve the curry with the remaining coriander sprinkled on top together with a drizzle of the reserved coconut milk.

**Serves 4**

*300g boneless chicken thighs, skin-on and cut into 3cm strips*

*2 tbsp vegetable oil*

*2 slices ginger, cut into matchsticks*

*1½ tbsp curry powder*

*2 medium floury potatoes (about 400g), peeled and cut into 2cm cubes*

*200g coconut milk*

*300ml chicken stock or water*

*20g lump of rock sugar or 2 tsp granulated sugar*

*handful fresh coriander, roughly chopped*

*salt*

*Sha cha* is an intensely savoury and slightly spicy sauce made from an aromatic combination of garlic, shallots, chilli and dried shrimp. Here it acts as a braising sauce but it can also be used as a punchy condiment (try it on noodles). At present you can only find *sha cha* sauce in the Chinese supermarket where it is often labelled 'BBQ sauce', so take the Chinese characters along with you to make sure you pick up the right jar (see page 261).

# sha cha chicken

1 Heat ½ tablespoon oil in a saucepan over a medium heat and fry the onion for 2 minutes until slightly softened. Remove and set aside.

2 Heat the remaining 1 tablespoon oil over a high heat and briefly fry the garlic and ginger until fragrant. Add the chicken and brown on all sides. While the chicken is browning, stir the *sha cha* sauce to ensure that the sediment is evenly distributed, then add it to the pan. Stir-fry to coat the chicken until you can see the oil separating from the sauce.

3 Pour 200ml water into the pan, add the salt and bamboo shoots and bring to a simmer. Cover, leaving the lid slightly ajar, and cook for 10 minutes until the sauce has thickened. Turn off the heat and mix in the spring onions. Just before serving, stir vigorously to emulsify the sauce.

**Serves 4**

1½ tbsp vegetable oil

½ medium onion (about 120g), sliced

2 cloves garlic, finely diced

1 tsp finely diced ginger

400g skinless, boneless chicken thighs, cut into 2cm strips

5 tbsp sha cha *sauce*

½ tsp salt

150g canned bamboo shoots, sliced

2 spring onions, diagonally sliced

If you are a fan of Peking duck pancakes, you will love this easy and deconstructed recipe for re-creating those flavours at home. The velvety duck meat is marinated with five-spice and stir-fried with the rich sauce that's usually spread on the pancakes, *tem meen jeung* (sweet bean sauce). Serve the duck with a light and spicy cucumber pickle – the perfect contrast in taste and texture to balance the intensity of the duck.

# duck and beansprout stir-fry with cucumber pickle

1   Start by removing the skin and fat from the duck breasts. Put the breast skin-side down on the board, hold the skin firmly on the left-hand side, then use a sharp knife angled at 45° to firmly scrape towards the right-hand side in the space between the fat and the meat. Slice the breast in half lengthways then slice on the diagonal into 1cm chunky pieces.

2   Put the duck in a bowl with all the marinade ingredients together with 2 teaspoons water. Cover and chill for 30 minutes.

3   Meanwhile, prepare the pickle. Combine the cucumber and remaining pickling ingredients in a bowl, cover and leave at room temperature.

4   Heat 1½ teaspoons vegetable oil in a wok over a medium-high heat. Add the duck and stir-fry for 3–4 minutes until cooked through and slightly singed at the edges. Transfer to a bowl and set aside.

5   Wipe the wok with kitchen paper, then put it over a medium heat. Add the remaining vegetable oil and stir-fry the garlic and beansprouts for 30 seconds. Sprinkle in 2 teaspoons water, cover and steam for 1 minute until the water has evaporated, then uncover, add the duck and sweet bean sauce and stir-fry for a further 2 minutes to warm through. To serve, drain the cucumber pickle and serve atop the duck and beansprouts.

**Serves 4**

2 duck breast fillets (about 400g)
3 tsp vegetable oil
1 clove garlic, thinly sliced
150g beansprouts
1 tbsp sweet bean sauce or hoisin sauce

**for the marinade**

1 tsp five-spice powder
¼ tsp salt
½ tsp granulated sugar
1 tsp vegetable oil
½ tsp cornflour
2 large pinches bicarbonate of soda

**for the pickle**

200g cucumber, deseeded and finely julienned
¼ tsp dried chilli flakes
pinch salt
2 tsp granulated sugar
3½ tsp Chinkiang vinegar
½ tsp sesame oil

As much as we obsess over Mum's Cracking Five-spiced Roast Pork Belly (page 186) with its light and airy crackling, we have always looked forward to 'the day after' when the crackling has inevitably lost its crunch. It's an unspoken practice in our family for any leftovers from roast day to be whipped up into this simple dish for the next evening's supper. As the pork belly bathes in a sweet soy sauce, the once-crispy crackling becomes slightly tacky to the bite while the sauce becomes infused with five-spice.

# five-spiced pork belly with spring onions and sweet soy

1   Mix all the sauce ingredients with 150ml water in a bowl, then set aside.

2   Put a medium-sized pan over a medium-high heat and fry the pork pieces cut-side down in a single layer until they are golden and singed like bacon. You should be able to see that some of the fat has rendered out. Flip the pork and keep sizzling until the underside is singed.

3   Add the ginger and stir-fry until fragrant, then reduce the heat to low, add the sauce mixture and cover. Simmer for 4–5 minutes, then uncover. As the sauce reduces and the sugar caramelises, it will turn dark and syrupy. At this stage, add the spring onions and 1 teaspoon water. Stir to wilt the spring onions slightly, then serve with the steamed rice.

**Serves 4**

*400g cooked Mum's Cracking Five-spiced Roast Pork (page 186), chopped into 2cm pieces*
*6 slices ginger, cut into matchsticks*
*10 spring onions, cut into 3cm lengths*
*steamed jasmine rice, to serve*

**for the sauce**
*2 tbsp light soy sauce*
*¼ tsp dark soy sauce*
*2 tbsp granulated sugar*

We fear that this recipe will be received with as much excitement as meatloaf – or even less, because at least meatloaf is baked. But please trust us: the combination of steam and simplicity definitely produces a winner here. You will get the best results by *dhuk*-ing (mincing) your own pork. All you need is a large sharp knife and a spare five minutes.

# gingery steamed pork patty

1  To *dhuk* the pork, cut it into small pieces and arrange in a single layer on the chopping board. Keeping the cleaver or knife edge parallel to the surface, work your way from one side of the layer of meat to the other with repeated chopping motions a few millimeters apart. Fold the pork over and keep *dhuk*-ing until it resembles a coarse mince.

2  Mix all the ingredients, except the ginger, with ½ tablespoon water in a bowl with a pair of chopsticks (or a fork) using a back and forth motion until just combined. Avoid stirring the pork as this will encourage the patty to become tough and springy.

3  Lightly oil a steam-proof dish and shape the pork into a rough patty. Leave dips and peaks on the surface so that cooking juices can pool in them. Scatter the ginger over the patty. If you are adding an exotic, dot the pieces of *harm yu* over the surface.

4  Steam for 10–15 minutes or until cooked through. You can test for this by poking a chopstick in the centre and having a peek inside: if no pink juices run out, it's done. Resist the urge to do this until the 10 minutes is up because the uncooked juices will clot and leave pools of gelatinous grey puddles on the surface. Serve piping hot.

**Serves 4**

*350g boneless pork shoulder*

*1 clove garlic, very finely diced*

*4 slices ginger, 1 very finely diced and 3 cut into fine matchsticks*

*¼ tsp salt*

*½ tsp granulated sugar*

*1 tsp light soy sauce*

*pinch ground white pepper*

*1 tbsp cornflour*

*½ tbsp vegetable oil, plus extra for oiling*

 **add an exotic (see page 14)**

*15g* harm yu *(salted fish), cut into pea-sized pieces*

These are our take on the beef schnitzel that Mum used to make for us when we were growing up. We have chosen pork to go with the ginger-laced, oil-kissed crispy coating, together with a simple but punchy orange sauce to add a citrusy finish. If you don't devour it all in one go; wedge some between thick slices of bread the next day for a scrummy lunch.

# zingy orange pork schnitzel

1   Cut the pork into 1cm thick slices. Pound each slice with a meat mallet or heavy rolling pin until it is about twice the size and 5mm thick. Transfer the pork to a bowl, add the marinade ingredients and 3 tablespoons water and mix thoroughly. Cover and chill for at least 1 hour.

2   Meanwhile, make the sauce. Heat the oil in a small saucepan over a medium heat. Gently fry the ginger for 2 minutes until slightly curled and lightly golden around the edges. Remove from the heat and leave to cool. Meanwhile, zest and peel the oranges. Blitz the flesh in a food processor to a paste. Add this along with the zest to the ginger with the remaining sauce ingredients and whisk over a low heat until thickened and almost translucent. Set aside.

3   Stir the beaten egg into the pork until the slices are coated. Put the cornflour into a large shallow dish or plate. Use one hand to lower a slice of pork onto the cornflour, and the other to firmly pat the cornflour over the entire surface of the pork slice. Repeat with the remaining slices.

4   Heat the oil for shallow-frying in a large frying pan over a medium heat and fry the pork for 3 minutes on each side until light golden. Remove and drain on kitchen paper. Serve the schnitzel sliced into strips, sprinkled with orange zest and the sauce in a bowl on the side.

**Serves 4**
400g boneless pork shoulder
grated zest of ½ orange
3 tbsp vegetable oil, for shallow-frying

**for the marinade**
1 clove garlic, very finely diced
½ tbsp ground ginger
½ tsp salt
¼ tbsp granulated sugar
1 tsp bicarbonate of soda
2 tbsp cornflour
1 tbsp light soy sauce
½ tbsp Shaoxing rice wine

**for the sauce**
2 tbsp vegetable oil
4 slices ginger, cut into matchsticks
2 oranges
pinch salt
2 tbsp granulated sugar
1 tbsp cornflour

**for the coating**
1 large egg, beaten
70g cornflour

At our family's market stall in Christchurch, our amazing little brother Justin holds down the 'buns and barbecue' side all by himself. Stroll past his floral gazebo and you will be instantly hooked by his chattiness and the tantalising aromas emanating off the grill. This recipe comes from the man himself, with a legendary satay sauce to boot. For the best results, start the evening beforehand so that the meat can marinate overnight.

# justin's beef kebab sticks with satay sauce

1  Mix the beef and all the marinade ingredients together in a large bowl. Stir in 90ml water, a little at a time. Cover and chill for at least 3 hours, ideally overnight.

2  For the satay sauce, heat all the ingredients in a saucepan over a medium-low heat, stirring continuously as the sauce comes to a gentle boil. Keep stirring until the sauce is thick and a dark orange colour. The sauce is ready when you can see a pool of red oil at the base of the saucepan. Cover and keep warm over the lowest heat while you get on with the kebabs.

3  Preheat the grill to its highest setting (240°C/475°F/Gas mark 9). If you are using bamboo or wooden skewers, soak them in water for 5 minutes (this will stop them burning on the grill). Thread 5–6 marinated cubes onto each skewer.

4  Heat a griddle pan on high heat and cook the beef for 3 minutes on one side before flipping over and cooking for a further 2 minutes. Transfer the kebabs to the grill for 1 minute on each side. To pan-fry: heat a little oil in a large frying pan over a high heat. Fry one side of the kebabs for 3 minutes, then flip over and fry the opposite side for 4 minutes. Give the satay sauce one last stir to distribute the oil throughout, then serve the kebabs with generous lashings of sauce and a sprinkling of coriander leaves.

Serves 4

400g beef rump steak, cut into 2cm chunks
vegetable oil, for cooking
fresh coriander leaves, for sprinkling

for the marinade
1 tsp bicarbonate of soda
1 tbsp vegetable oil
¾ tbsp light soy sauce
¼ tsp dark soy sauce
¼ tsp salt
¼ tsp ground white pepper
2 tbsp granulated sugar
1 tbsp cornflour

for the satay sauce
400ml coconut cream
½ tbsp salt
2 tbsp soft dark brown sugar
1 tbsp chilli powder
3 tbsp curry powder
4 tbsp dried breadcrumbs
2 tbsp crunchy peanut butter
30g roasted peanuts, finely chopped
75g granulated sugar
1 tbsp vegetable oil

Feeling tense and dreading the idea of having to cook dinner? If so, this is the dish for you. The best part of putting these meatballs together is that you literally get to throw them around, releasing any pent up frustrations in the process. It's this very technique that gives Chinese meatballs such a special mouthfeel. In contrast to Italian-style meatballs, the hallmark of these *ow yook yuen* is a surprisingly *daan* (springy) and *waat* (smooth) texture.

# aromatic steamed beef meatballs

1   Use one hand to fold together the beef, bicarbonate of soda and egg in a large bowl until well combined. Form the beef into a ball inside the bowl, then pick up the ball and hold it about 30cm away from the bowl. *Daat* the meat, which means to throw it with force into the bowl so that you hear a crisp slapping sound. Have some fun *daat*-ing the meat 30 times.

2   Add the water chestnuts, coriander, 2 tablespoons water and all the marinade ingredients to the meat. Use a pair of chopsticks to vigorously stir the contents of the bowl in one direction (e.g. clockwise). Notice how the mince starts to take on a smoother and paste-like consistency. At this point, *daat* the mixture 10 more times. Cover and leave to marinate in the fridge for at least 1 hour.

3   To prepare the meatballs, wet your hands and roll the mixture into 16 balls. Try to compact the balls as tightly as you can so that they will retain their shape while steaming.

4   Lightly oil a steam-proof plate. Steam the meatballs in three batches over vigorously boiling water for 8 minutes per batch. Devour each batch as soon as it comes out of the steamer with a generous splash of Worcestershire sauce on top.

**Makes 16**

*400g lean beef mince*
*¾ tsp bicarbonate of soda*
*1 large egg*
*40g water chestnuts, drained and roughly diced*
*40g fresh coriander, roughly chopped*
*vegetable oil, for oiling*
*Worcestershire sauce, to serve*

**for the marinade**

*1 tbsp cornflour*
*pinch salt*
*¼ tsp ground white pepper*
*½ tsp granulated sugar*
*½ tbsp Shaoxing rice wine*
*¾ tsp sesame oil*
*½ tbsp vegetable oil, plus extra for oiling*
*1 tsp light soy sauce*
*½ tbsp finely diced ginger*

It's no exaggeration to say that these ribs are insanely mouthwatering. If you're like us, your stomach will grumble longingly when the aroma wafts from the oven, before your heart rate quickens at the sight of deep red, sticky ribs that are so highly varnished they have the light-reflecting sheen of toffee apples. The secret is to lovingly and patiently paint on layers upon layers of extra hoisin and honey . . . before you take to devouring them rather animalistically that is!

# lacquered honey hoisin pork spare ribs

1    Slice the rack into individual ribs then rinse them thoroughly under cold water. Drain, then pop the ribs into a large bowl together with the marinade ingredients. Use your hands to massage the marinade into the ribs. Cover and chill for at least 30 minutes.

2    Preheat the oven to 220°C/425°F/Gas mark 7. Line a baking tray with foil. Mix the hoisin sauce and oil in a small bowl so that it is ready for basting later on.

3    Arrange the marinated ribs on the tray in a single layer, sitting them up on their sides (cut sides facing up and down) and bake for 5 minutes on each side. Liberally brush the hoisin and oil mixture over the ribs and bake for a further 8–9 minutes on each side until the ribs have dried out and become slightly singed. Brush half of the honey over the ribs and bake for a further 2 minutes before removing the ribs from the oven and brushing the remaining honey on top. They should be glistening and very sticky by this point.

4    To serve, pile the ribs onto a plate and have wet wipes at the ready.

Serves 4
*800g rack of pork ribs*

**for the marinade**
*1½ tbsp hoisin sauce*
*2 cloves garlic, very finely diced*
*2 tsp Shaoxing rice wine*
*2 pinches salt*
*½ tsp bicarbonate of soda*
*2 tsp cornflour*

**for the basting**
*1½ tbsp hoisin sauce*
*½ tsp vegetable oil*
*1½ tbsp runny honey*

Water spinach, or *tong choi*, has little in common with ordinary spinach and in our opinion, is a much more exciting vegetable to eat. *Tong choi* is most adored for its stem: long tubes with thin walls (just like drinking straws) that remain crunchy when cooked. It can be a bit pricey at the Chinese supermarket, but if you spot some and have never had it before, we encourage you to give it a try.

# stir-fried water spinach

1   If you are adding an exotic: mash the *four yu* into a paste in a small bowl and set aside.

2   Rinse the water spinach thoroughly then cut into 8cm lengths. Leave to air-dry in a colander for up to 30 minutes if you have the time.

3   Heat the oil in a wok or in a large frying pan over a high heat and cook the garlic for about 20 seconds. Add the water spinach and stir-fry for 2 minutes until the leaves have just started to wilt.

4   Add the sugar and salt or *four yu* paste, if using, and stir-fry for 1 minute until the stalks are just cooked but still very crunchy. Serve immediately.

DUMPLING SISTERS TIP
*Four yu* (fermented beancurd) is salty on its own so if you are using it in the recipe, omit the salt. It also works well in stir-fries with other leafy green vegetables, such as *choi sum* or spinach, but not with vegetables that have a high water content, such as pak choi.

**Serves 4**
*370g water spinach*
*2 tbsp vegetable oil*
*3 cloves garlic, quartered and smashed*
*½ tsp granulated sugar*
*¼ tsp salt*

**add an exotic (see page 14)**
*3 cubes four yu (fermented bean curd), see also tip*

If you have never eaten cooked cucumber before, the idea of eating it hot might seem strange. Yet the extraordinary thing about stir-fried cucumber is that it readily absorbs flavours and retains a *waat* (silky and slippery) texture that provides a very satisfying bite.

# stir-fried cucumber

1   Cut the cucumbers in half lengthways, then use a spoon to scrape out the seeds. Cut each half into four strips lengthways, then divide each of these strips into batons, about 4cm long.

2   Mix the cucumber and salt together in a large bowl, then set aside for 10 minutes. Rinse the cucumber batons thoroughly, shaking off any excess water and pat dry with kitchen paper.

3   Heat the vegetable oil in a wok over a high heat and stir-fry the ginger and garlic until fragrant, then add the cucumber. Stir-fry for 1 minute then stir in the sugar and chilli flakes. Spread the cucumber out in a single layer on the base of the wok, and leave them to singe for 30 seconds. Stir-fry for a few seconds then spread the cucumber out again and leave to singe again for 30 seconds. Sprinkle 1 teaspoon water over the cucumber then stir-fry for another minute. Remove from the heat, stir in the sesame oil, then serve.

**Serves 4**
2 cucumbers
½ tsp salt
2 tsp vegetable oil
2 tsp finely diced ginger
2 cloves garlic, finely diced
½ tsp granulated sugar
¼ tsp dried chilli flakes
¼ tsp sesame oil

Our Dad is quite the gardener and one of his proudest crops is his thriving mangetout. So thriving, in fact, that we have had to start selling them at the market. The best way to enjoy mangetout is by stir-frying them quickly over super-high heat. Here, seasonings are kept simple so that the *cheow* (refreshingly crisp) mouthfeel of the mangetout really stands out.

# stir-fried mangetout

1   Heat the oil in a wok over a high heat. If you are adding an exotic: add the *larp cheong* and stir-fry until it is slightly blistered.

2   Add the mangetout, salt, pepper and ginger. Stir-fry for 1 minute then serve piping hot.

**Serves 4**
1½ tsp vegetable oil
250g mangetout
pinch salt
pinch ground white pepper
1 tsp finely diced ginger

 **add an exotic (see page 14)**
*60g larp cheong (Chinese sausage), diagonally sliced*

Growing up, this was one of the most frequent veg dishes that showed up on our family table. Mum knew that the vermicelli had a brilliant ability to soak up flavours while remaining delectably *waat* (slippery), so it was the perfect partner to the crunch of Chinese leaf. Simple and cleansing, this dish is truly 'everyday' – the Chinese equivalent of a trusty salad.

# vermicelli and chinese leaf

1   Soak the vermicelli in cold water for 10 minutes, then drain. If adding an exotic: soak the *har mey* in hot water for 30 minutes, then drain.

2   Peel the leaves off the Chinese cabbage and wash them in several changes of water. Slice each in half lengthways, then into wide diagonal strips. Set aside.

3   Heat ½ tablespoon vegetable oil in a medium saucepan over a medium-high heat and fry the ginger and spring onions until they are fragrant and the spring onions wilted slightly. Add ¼ teaspoon salt and the *har mey* (if using) and stir briefly, then pour in 250ml hot water. Cover and let the mixture bubble furiously for 3 minutes. Reduce the heat to low and stir in the pepper and sugar.

4   Drain the vermicelli and add it to the saucepan, stirring to coat it in the liquid. Partially cover and leave to slowly come up to a simmer until the liquid is all absorbed.

5   Meanwhile, heat the remaining ½ tablespoon vegetable oil in a large frying pan and lightly fry the garlic for about 30 seconds. Add the cabbage and toss to coat in the garlicky oil and stir-fry until the white stems are almost translucent but still crunchy and the leaves have collapsed. Season with the remaining ¼ teaspoon salt.

6   Add the sesame oil and 2 tablespoons hot water to the vermicelli to loosen it, if needed, then add the cabbage, mix to combine and serve.

**Serves 4**

*50g dried bean thread vermicelli*

*½ large Chinese leaf cabbage (about 330g)*

*1 tbsp vegetable oil*

*4 slices ginger, cut into matchsticks*

*2 spring onions, cut in half then divided into 5cm long sections*

*½ tsp salt*

*large pinch ground white pepper*

*¼ tsp granulated sugar*

*1 clove garlic, finely diced*

*1 tsp sesame oil*

 **add an exotic (see page 14)**

*1 tbsp har mey (dried shrimp)*

Back home in Christchurch, New Zealand, there's a legendary Chinese farmer who is known city-wide for his ability to grow the X-Men of vegetables: produce so ridiculously sturdy and good looking that one has to wonder if they are mutants (in a good way). His Chinese broccoli (*gai lan*) is the most impressive offering of all. There's no better way to enjoy this veg than by stir-frying it rapidly with a touch of rice wine. You can substitute the *gai lan* with broccolini, if you prefer.

# cantonese stir-fried chinese broccoli

1 Bring about 1.4 litres water to the boil in a large saucepan. Rip the leaves from the central stalk of each *gai lan* plant. For larger leaves that have a longer stem, rip off the stem as well and tear the leaves in half. Cut the stalks at an angle into chopstickable pieces. Add the bicarbonate of soda to the boiling water, then blanch the *gai lan* for 1–2 minutes, or until just soft. Immediately drain in a colander.

2 In a bowl, mix the cornflour and 2 teaspoons water into a slurry then set aside.

3 Heat a wok or large frying pan over a high heat. Add the oil and stir-fry the ginger until fragrant. Add the *gai lan* and stir-fry quickly. Add the rice wine, salt and sugar and stir-fry for 2 minutes or until you can smell the rice wine. Stir the cornflour slurry briefly then add it to the wok and toss until each piece of *gai lan* is glossy, and serve.

**Serves 4**

*300g Chinese broccoli (gai lan)*
*¼ tsp bicarbonate of soda*
*½ tsp cornflour*
*1 tbsp vegetable oil*
*2 tsp finely diced ginger*
*2 tsp Shaoxing rice wine*
*½ tsp salt*
*½ tsp granulated sugar*

The secret of cooking aubergine is to use methods that encourage the spongy white flesh to drink up strong flavours while cooking down to a succulent and *waat* (silky) texture. The 'fish fragrant' preparation hails from the Sichuanese tradition, named as such not to describe the use of fish, but because the seasoning (a harmonious balance of salty, sweet, spicy and sour) has long been used to cleverly undercut the overly fishy aroma when cooking with less than perfect fish.

# 'fish fragrant' aubergine

1   Trim the aubergines, then cut them in half lengthways. Put one aubergine half horizontally on the chopping board with the cut side facing up and cut it into chunky shards by pivoting the knife by about 45° after each cut. Repeat with the remaining aubergine.

2   In a bowl, mix the cornflour and 1½ tablespoons water into a slurry and set aside. If the chilli bean sauce is chunky, roughly chop it so there are no large pieces then mix it with the remaining sauce ingredients in a small bowl and set aside.

3   Heat 2 tablespoons oil in a wok over a medium heat. Add the aubergine and stir-fry for 2 minutes. Add the remaining oil, then flip the aubergine only every few seconds for the next 3–4 minutes giving them a chance to cook through and blisters slightly. Add the sauce and stir–fry for 30 seconds, then reduce the heat slightly, pour in 60ml water and simmer for 2 minutes.

4   Reduce the heat to the lowest setting then stir in the cornflour slurry. Increase the heat to medium, then toss in the vinegar and the spring onions. Stir-fry for 1 minute, then serve.

**Serves 4**

*2 large aubergines*
*1½ tsp cornflour*
*3 tbsp vegetable oil*
*1½ tsp Chinkiang vinegar*
*2 spring onions, sliced*

**for the sauce**

*1½ tbsp chilli bean sauce*
*5 cloves garlic, finely diced*
*2½ tsp finely diced ginger*
*1½ tsp cracked Sichuan*
*   peppercorns*
*1 tsp light soy sauce*
*2 pinches salt*
*2 tsp granulated sugar*

You have not tasted the true potential of the humble green bean until you've tried this classic and *wok hei*-infused Sichuanese dish. The key is the 'dry-frying' technique: rapid tossing of the raw beans in hot oil until they begin to blister. We source traditional yard-long beans because they are more robust than other varieties, but French beans would do the trick too. Be sure to include the Chinese mushrooms – their fleshiness and *daan* (springy) mouthfeel adds a delightful extra layer of texture to the dish.

# spicy blistered beans

1 Soak the Chinese mushrooms in a bowl of hot water with the sugar for 20 minutes, then drain. Remove and discard the stalks and finely dice the caps. Mix the mushrooms and seasoning ingredients together in a small bowl and set aside.

2 If the chilli bean sauce is chunky, chop it roughly so there are no large pieces, then mix it with the remaining sauce ingredients and 2 tablespoons water and set aside.

3 Rinse the beans and use kitchen paper to pat them dry. If you are using yard-long beans, cut them into 8–10cm lengths.

4 Heat 2 tablespoons oil in the wok over a medium-high heat. Add the beans and stir-fry for 5–6 minutes or until they are slightly blistered and softened but not limp. Remove the beans and drain on a double layer of kitchen paper.

5 Add 2 teaspoons oil to the wok and stir-fry the mushrooms and seasoning mixture over a medium heat for 30 seconds, until the spices are fragrant. Turn off the heat and rest for 2 minutes before stirring in the sauce mixture.

6 Return the wok to a medium heat and when the sauce starts to sizzle, add the beans and stir-fry for 1 minute until the beans are warm and coated with the sauce. Serve immediately.

**Serves 4**

*4 dried Chinese mushrooms*
*2 pinches granulated sugar*
*400g yard-long or French beans, trimmed*
*vegetable oil, for cooking*

**for the seasoning**

*2 cloves garlic, finely diced*
*1 tbsp very finely diced ginger*
*4 spring onions, white parts only, finely sliced*
*½ tsp cracked Sichuan peppercorns*
*¼ tsp dried chilli flakes or 1 whole dried chilli, sliced into rounds*

**for the sauce**

*3 tsp chilli bean sauce*
*2 tsp Shaoxing rice wine*
*½ tsp salt*
*1½ tsp granulated sugar*

In Cantonese, *larp jarp* means miscellaneous. The best thing about this dish with six miscellaneous veg is that it is so much more than the sum of its parts: the core ingredients come together in a wonderful burst of colour, and it is propelled far beyond the 'boring veg' category by the addition of a little luxury in the form of fragrant pine nuts.

# rainbow vegetable medley

1   Fill a small saucepan with enough oil to a depth of 2cm and put over a medium heat. To test that the oil is ready, drop in a single pine nut. It should fizz up, but not turn brown instantly. Carefully lower the pine nuts into the hot oil and deep-fry for 1–2 minutes. Keep a really close eye on them, because they will change from pale to golden very quickly and can rapidly burn. As soon as they smell fragrant and have turned golden, remove and drain on kitchen paper.

2   In a small bowl, mix all the sauce ingredients with 100ml water and set aside.

3   Heat ½ tablespoon oil in a wok over a high heat and stir-fry the ginger, garlic and carrots until fragrant. Sprinkle 1½ tablespoons cold water on top and cover. Steam for 1–2 minutes, or until the water has evaporated and the carrots have softened.

4   Add the peas, courgette, drained sweetcorn and red pepper together with another ½ tablespoon oil and stir-fry for 1 minute. Add 1 table-spoon water and cover. Uncover after 1 minute and allow any remaining water to evaporate. Reduce the heat to the lowest setting and gradually stir in the sauce. Increase the heat to medium. When the sauce has thickened, stir in two-thirds of the fried pine nuts. Serve with the remaining pine nuts sprinkled on top.

**Serves 4**

*1 tbsp vegetable oil, plus extra for deep-frying*

*4 tbsp pine nuts*

*1 tsp finely diced ginger*

*1 clove garlic, finely diced*

*1 large carrot (70g), chopped into pea-sized dices*

*70g frozen peas*

*½ medium courgette (about 60g), chopped into pea-sized dices*

*110g canned sweetcorn (drained weight)*

*½ red pepper (about 80g), chopped into pea-sized dices*

**for the sauce**

*1½ tsp light soy sauce*

*2 pinches ground white pepper*

*¼ tbsp cornflour*

*salt*

oodles of noodles

Noodles are at least 6,000 years old and the reason they have hung around for so long is not rocket science: they are simply fantastic. Fantastic ropes for flavour to cling to; fantastic tangles that don't need untangling before eating; fantastic company to curl up on the couch with, and fantastically fun to eat (or slurp, or inhale).

For the Chinese, noodles are also thought to bring good fortune since long strands of noodles symbolise long life. To get a yearly fix of this gastronomic elixir of life, birthday boys and girls (and grandpas and grannies) eat 'longevity noodles' where the trick is to pick up and eat the noodles without breaking or biting them (chewing is okay and recommended).

On an everyday basis, we are more concerned with making noodles as delicious as possible and we hope you will find that every recipe in this chapter achieves just that. To showcase the fabulous variety of Chinese noodles we include a mixture of noodles prepared in different ways: *chao meen sup* (stir-fried wet) or *chao meen ghun* (stir-fried dry), *lo meen* (stirred with a sauce), *yeung meen* (simmered in a sauce), *tong mien* (with soup), and *ja meen* (eh hmm, deep-fried).

If you love noodles as much we do, you will soon find ways to eat them at all times of the day, even at breakfast or as a naughty, fritter-ised snack.

These noodles are a bestseller at the market and the recipe has barely changed in 20 years. We keep the vegetables simple – carrots, cabbage and broccoli, each with their distinct shape, colour and texture – to enhance the star of the show: the noodles. Our secret for creating juicy noodles without ladles of oil is simple: create a quick one-wok chicken gravy so that every strand of noodle is coated with a light but delicious slick of sauce.

# market chicken fried noodles

1   Mix the chicken, marinade ingredients and 2 tablespoons water together in a bowl. Cover and leave to marinate for 20 minutes.

2   Prepare the dried egg noodles according to the packet instructions, reducing the cooking time by a half. Drain in a colander and use a pair of scissors to cut through the pile of noodles to shorten them.

3   Heat 2 tablespoons oil in a wok over a high heat and stir-fry half of the ginger and garlic until fragrant. Add the marinated chicken, spread it over the base in a single layer and allow to brown for 1 minute, then flip the chicken every 30 seconds for a further 3 minutes, or until the chicken pieces have a golden crust.

4   Pour in 60ml water, cover with a lid or plate and leave for 1 minute until the chicken is cooked through. Transfer the chicken, gravy and any sticky brown bits to a bowl and set aside.

5   Wipe the wok with kitchen paper. Heat 1 tablespoon oil over a high heat and stir-fry the remaining ginger and garlic. Add the carrot slices, cabbage and broccoli and toss the vegetables in the oil for 1 minute, before pouring in 80ml water and covering with a lid. This traps in the *wok hei* (the smoky flavours or 'breath' of the wok). Cook for 2 minutes until the vegetables have softened, then uncover and reduce the heat to medium-low.

6   Return the chicken and gravy to the wok, together with the noodles, salt, sugar, dark soy sauce and the remaining 1 tablespoon oil. Toss the noodles until they are evenly coated and warmed through. Serve with chilli sauce, if that's your style.

**Serves 4**

*300g skinless, boneless chicken thighs, cut into strips*
*250g dried egg noodles*
*4 tbsp vegetable oil*
*1 tbsp finely diced ginger*
*1 clove garlic, finely diced*
*1 small carrot, thinly sliced*
*½ small white cabbage (about 260g), roughly shredded*
*½ head of a medium broccoli, cut into florets*
*¾ tsp salt*
*1¼ tsp granulated sugar*
*1 tsp dark soy sauce*
*chilli sauce, to serve (optional)*

**for the marinade**
*½ tsp light soy sauce*
*¼ tsp salt*
*¼ tsp granulated sugar*
*pinch ground white pepper*
*1 tsp cornflour*
*¼ tsp bicarbonate of soda*

This is an assemble-and-eat dish that is light and fresh but still big on flavour. In this salad, the chicken breast is a great texture contrast against the slippery noodles and *cheow* (crunchy) mangetout. This is the perfect light meal for a warm night, a great partner for the main event at summer barbecues and a tasty option for packed lunches.

# peanutty chicken vermicelli salad

1   If you are adding an exotic: pan-fry the *har mey* in the oil until crunchy. Drain on kitchen paper and set aside.

2   Soak the vermicelli in hot water for 5–10 minutes until the strands are translucent and soft but not gloopy. Tip into a colander, rinse under cold water and set aside.

3   Put the shredded chicken and all the chicken sauce ingredients into a small saucepan. Pour in 120ml water and cook over a low heat until all the liquid has been absorbed.

4   Mix the dressing ingredients together in a small bowl and set aside.

5   Put the vermicelli, chicken, peanuts, mangetout, coriander, and *har mey*, if using, into a large bowl and pour the dressing over the top. Gently toss the salad, coating the vermicelli with the dressing and serve.

**Serves 2 as a main, 4 as a side dish**

*100g dried bean thread vermicelli*

*1 large cooked skinless chicken breast, shredded*

*6½ tbsp roasted peanuts, finely chopped*

*50g mangetout, sliced*

*2 tbsp roughly chopped fresh coriander*

**for the chicken sauce**

*1 tsp light soy sauce*

*¼ tsp dark soy sauce*

*pinch ground white pepper*

**for the salad dressing**

*¼ tsp dried chilli flakes*

*1½ tsp finely diced ginger*

*½ tbsp light soy sauce*

*¼ tsp dark soy sauce*

*1½ tsp sesame oil*

*1 tbsp Chinkiang vinegar*

*pinch salt*

*pinch ground white pepper*

*1 tsp granulated sugar*

 **add an exotic (see page 14)**

*1 tbsp har mey (dried shrimp)*

*2 tsp vegetable oil*

Picture this familiar scene: you have just arrived home after a long day and you are so ravenous that the mere thought of lifting a finger to raw ingredients instantly saps what little remains in your energy reserves. So you reach into the back of the cupboard for a crushed packet of instant noodles, or perhaps you start dreaming of takeaways . . . but wait! These almost-instant noodles are a brilliant home-cooked option: nutritious, tasty, cost-effective and very much in the spirit of 'throw it together'.

# almost-instant chicken noodle soup

1   Stir the chicken, salt, pepper, cornflour, bicarbonate of soda and 2 teaspoons water together in a small bowl.

2   Heat the oil in saucepan over a medium heat, add the ginger and allow it to sizzle for 30 seconds before adding the chicken. Brown the chicken for 1 minute, then add 350ml boiling water. Cover immediately and keep the broth cooking on a gentle rolling boil for 4–5 minutes.

3   Pop the noodles into the stock, and as soon as they can be loosened with a pair of chopsticks (before they are completely soft), add the choi sum. Reduce the heat to low and simmer until the noodles are al dente and the choi sum has wilted. Serve in a large bowl with a dollop of chilli sauce.

**Serves 1**

*1 chicken breast, thinly sliced*
*¼ tsp salt*
*2 pinches ground white pepper*
*½ tsp cornflour*
*¼ tsp bicarbonate of soda*
*1 tsp vegetable oil*
*2 slices ginger, cut into matchsticks*
*65g dried egg noodles or 1 instant noodle nest*
*150g choi sum, pak choi or Chinese leaf cabbage, roughly chopped*
*½ tsp chilli sauce, to serve*

Oyster sauce is a brilliantly versatile concoction, often used sparingly in Cantonese cooking to add greater depth to many dishes. This recipe celebrates the pure flavour of oyster sauce by coating egg noodles rather luxuriously with it. Crisp broccoli florets balance out the richness of the sauce, while the fried onions add a bit of cheeky indulgence.

# broccoli oyster sauce noodles with fried onions

1 Pour the oil into a saucepan to a depth of 1cm and put it over a high heat. In a bowl, massage the pepper into the sliced onion. To test that the oil is ready, drop a small piece of onion into it. It should fizz up, but not turn brown immediately.

2 Add the cornflour to the onion and use your fingers to ensure the onion is well coated. Add the onion slices to the hot oil. Lower the heat to medium, then use a pair of chopsticks to loosen the onions so that they don't clump together. Fry for about 4 minutes until crisp and golden brown. Carefully remove and drain on kitchen paper.

3 Fill a large saucepan two-thirds of the way up with boiling water, place it over a medium heat and add the noodles. As soon as you can loosen the noodles with chopsticks, push them to one side and nestle the broccoli in the free space. Cook on a rolling boil for a further 2–3 minutes.

4 Meanwhile, put all the sauce ingredients into a small saucepan along with 120ml water. Simmer gently until the liquid has reduced by half.

5 Set aside a third of the sauce in a bowl, then drain the noodles and add to the reduced sauce. Toss the noodles in the sauce, then transfer them to two large plates. For a classically Cantonese presentation, tuck the broccoli florets (stem side in) all the way around the outside of the noodle nests. Drizzle the remaining sauce around the edge of the broccoli and sprinkle the fried onions and chilli, if using, on top.

**Serves 2**

vegetable oil, for shallow-frying
2 pinches ground white pepper
1 onion, thinly sliced
½ tbsp cornflour
125g dried egg noodles
1 small broccoli, cut into florets
1 fresh red chilli, thinly sliced, to serve (optional)

**for the sauce**
120ml oyster sauce
2 pinches salt
2 spring onions, thinly sliced

We enjoy deep-fried wontons as much as the next *wei sic mao* (affectionately hungry cat), but wontons in noodle soup really live up to their name: wonton literally means 'to swallow a cloud'. Traditional wonton shops in Hong Kong make mind-blowingly flavoursome broths with dried fish, pig trotters, pork neck bones and Jinhua dry-cured ham. To keep things simple, we make our delicious savoury broth with just a few easily sourced ingredients.

# wonton noodle soup

1  For the broth, rinse the ribs and chicken carcasses in water then put into a large stockpot, together with the bacon and *har mey*, if using. Cover with boiling water and bring to the boil vigorously for 5 minutes, then discard the water. Refill the stockpot with 2.5 litres boiling water. Add the ginger, cover, place over a medium heat and cook on a gentle rolling boil for at least 2 hours.

2  Chop the pork into small pieces then *dhuk* (chop repeatedly with force) until it resembles coarse mince. Pop the pork into a large bowl together with the remaining filling ingredients, except the prawns, and use a pair of chopsticks to stir vigorously in one direction (e.g. clockwise) until the meat binds to itself. Cover and chill for at least 30 minutes, then stir in the prawns.

3  Fill a small bowl with cold water. Cradle a wrapper in one hand, and use a finger to slightly wet all four edges of the wrapper. Place a heaped teaspoon of filling in the centre of the wrapper, then fold it over and press the edges firmly together to form a triangle. Press in as close as possible to the filling when you are pressing the edges of the wrapper together so that there are no air pockets. Dab a little water on the left and right corners (the 'wings') of the triangle, then pull these corners downwards towards each other. Cross the tip of one wing slightly over the top of the other one and pinch firmly to seal. Keep the wontons covered to prevent them drying out.

**Serves 4**

20 wonton wrappers
250g fresh wonton noodles
   or 200g dried egg noodles
180g Chinese leaf cabbage,
   roughly chopped
3 spring onions, thinly sliced
200g sliced Char Siu Pork
   (page 189), to serve
Chinkiang vinegar, to serve

**for the broth**

350g loose pork ribs
2 chicken carcasses, halved
200g unsmoked back bacon,
   fat removed
3 slices ginger

**for the filling**

200g boneless pork shoulder
40g canned bamboo shoots,
   finely diced
2 tsp finely diced ginger
1 clove garlic, finely diced
¼ tsp salt
¼ tsp granulated sugar
pinch ground white pepper
¼ tsp sesame oil
¼ tsp bicarbonate of soda
1 tsp cornflour
40g raw king prawns, peeled
   and roughly chopped

*(continues overleaf)*

4  Fill a large saucepan two-thirds with hot water and bring to the boil. Slip the wontons into the pan and wait for the water to come to the boil again, then pour in 250ml cold water and add the dried egg noodles, if using. Wait for the water to come to the boil, then add another 250ml cold water (together with the fresh wonton noodles, if using). When the water starts boiling again, reduce the heat to a gentle rolling boil, add the cabbage, and cook for 1 minute. Serve the wontons, noodles and vegetables in big soup bowls with the aromatic broth poured over, a sprinkling of spring onions, Char Siu pork slices and, if you like, a dash of vinegar.

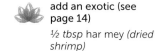

**add an exotic (see page 14)**
½ tbsp har mey (dried shrimp)

DUMPLING SISTERS TIP
If the broth seems too oily, simply skim off the top layer after it has finished cooking. Alternatively, you can line a bowl with kitchen paper then ladle the oily bits on top (the paper will catch any oil). Simply gather up the kitchen paper and discard it before pouring the skimmed broth back into the stockpot. You can transfer the broth to an airtight container and freeze it for up to two months.

In the perpetually heaving 'kitchen' of one of the tiniest ramshackle restaurants near our uncle Bak Yeh's apartment in Guangzhou, huge plastic platefuls of the most brilliant *ow ho fun* is dished out to hungry locals. This lusciously dark rice noodle dish is a Cantonese lunchtime staple, adored for its simplicity and smoky flavour. You will be surprised at how easy it is to whip up an authentic *ow ho* at home.

# beef fried rice noodles

1  Mix the beef, marinade ingredients and 2 teaspoons water together in a bowl, cover and chill for at least 30 minutes.

2  Rinse the rice noodles under cold water to remove some of the starch, then put them in a large baking dish or tray with high sides and cover them completely with boiling water. Soak for 10 minutes then tip them into a colander. The noodles should be slightly softened but still firm.

3  Mix all the pre-mix seasoning ingredients with 2 tablespoons water in a small bowl and set aside. Slice the whites of the spring onions through lengthways, then cut both white and green parts into 5cm-long segments.

4  Heat 1½ teaspoons oil in the wok over a high heat and stir-fry the beef until it is cooked right through with a golden crust on the outside, then remove it from the wok and set aside.

5  We suggest cooking the noodles in two batches for easier tossing. With the wok still on high heat, add 1 teaspoon oil and half of the beansprouts and stir-fry for 30 seconds. Add half of the softened rice noodles and half of the pre-mix seasoning, and use a spatula to fold the seasoning into the noodles. Have a nibble on a noodle to check for softness – if it is too hard for your liking, keep sprinkling cold water onto the noodles and toss until they soften. Add half of the cooked beef and half of the spring onions, and toss the noodles one more time to soften the spring onions. Repeat with the remaining half of the ingredients, then serve.

**Serves 4**

200g beef rump steak, sliced against the grain into thin strips
600g dried wide rice noodles
8 spring onions
3½ tsp vegetable oil
200g beansprouts

**for the marinade**
¼ tsp bicarbonate of soda
½ tsp cornflour
½ tsp light soy sauce
¼ tsp salt
½ tsp granulated sugar
¼ tsp ground white pepper
1 tsp vegetable oil

**for the pre-mix seasoning**
2 tbsp dark soy sauce
2 tsp salt
½ tsp ground white pepper
1 tbsp vegetable oil

If there is one word that embodies these noodles, it's lush. Lush in its juicy bite, lush in its alluring dark colour, and lush in its indulgent assortment of ingredients. The cooking technique is an example of *yeung mian* (literally, 'to stuff noodles') where the noodles are gently simmered in a flavoursome liquid until plump and piping hot. The result is a tangle of resplendently saucy – not soupy – noodles that are themselves saturated in flavour.

# hokkien noodles

1  Mix the salt, sugar, cornflour and chicken together in a bowl. Combine the sauce ingredients with 200ml water in another bowl.

2  Heat 1 tablespoon oil in a wok or large frying pan over a high heat and stir-fry the ginger and garlic until fragrant. Add the chicken and spread it out in a single layer. When the chicken starts to lift off without too much prodding, stir-fry for 3 minutes, or until it is almost cooked through. Add the prawns and fish balls and stir-fry until the prawns have just turned pink. Remove and set aside.

3  Heat 1 tablespoon oil in the wok, add the carrot slices and toss to coat in the oil. Sprinkle in 1 tablespoon water and stir-fry for a minute until the carrots have softened slightly. Add the choi sum and stir-fry until the leaves have started to wilt.

4  Reduce the heat to medium-low and add the noodles to the wok together with the cooked chicken and seafood, sauce mixture and spring onion. Allow to simmer very gently, occasionally turning the noodles until most of the liquid has been absorbed and the noodles are a luscious dark colour and piping hot.

DUMPLING SISTERS TIP
Fish balls are wonderfully *daan ngaa* (springy) and great for sinking your teeth into – you will find them in the freezer section of Chinese supermarkets.

**Serves 4–6**

*pinch salt*
*¼ tsp granulated sugar*
*¼ tsp cornflour*
*180g skinless, boneless chicken thighs, cut into 2cm-thick slices*
*2½ tbsp vegetable oil*
*2 slices ginger, sliced into matchsticks*
*1 clove garlic, thinly sliced*
*100g raw king prawns, peeled*
*3 fish balls (see tip), quartered*
*½ medium carrot (about 40g), halved lengthways and sliced*
*200g choi sum, chopped into 5cm lengths*
*300g fresh egg noodles*
*1 spring onion, halved lengthways and sliced into thirds*

**for the sauce**
*1 tbsp light soy sauce*
*1¼ tsp dark soy sauce*
*¼ tsp ground white pepper*
*½ tsp granulated sugar*

The intensely savoury and potent meat sauce in this dish comes about from the 'frying' of three different bean-based sauces. All of the sauces are used in northern Chinese cooking, and most often you will see recipes for *ja jeung meen* cooked in the Beijing or Shanghai style. We have made it here to the Hong Kong style, which is more red in colour and slightly tangy. Because the meat is such an important part of the sauce, use a fattier cut such as belly or shoulder as this will contribute a more luxurious flavour and mouthfeel.

# fried sauce noodles

1   Cut the pork into roughly 2cm cubes then use a cleaver or heavy knife to *dhuk* or grind the pork into little pieces until it resembles coarse mince. Mix the pork with the cornflour, 2 teaspoons water and the bicarbonate of soda and leave to marinate for 15 minutes.

2   Heat 2 teaspoons oil in a wok or frying pan over a medium heat and stir-fry the ginger and garlic until fragrant. Add the pork and brown (you may need an extra teaspoon or two of oil if you are using lean pork mince), then remove and set aside.

3   If your chilli bean sauce has large pieces in it, roughly chop it until it resembles a rough paste. Heat 1 tablespoon oil in the wok or frying pan over a medium heat. Spoon in the yellow soybean and sweet bean pastes along with the chilli bean sauce, swirl together and fry for 2–3 minutes until fragrant and the pastes start to form clumps that blister on the surface.

4   Return the pork to the pan and add the tomato ketchup and 250ml water. Loosen any large clumps of paste. Bring to the boil before reducing the heat and simmering for 10 minutes, uncovered, until the sauce has thickened and the pork is deep red. You may need to add some more water. Stir in the vinegar, if using.

5   Cook the noodles in a pan of boiling water according to the packet instructions, drain and stir in a few drops of cooking oil to prevent the noodles from sticking. Serve the sauce on top of the noodles.

**Serves 2**

*300g pork shoulder or belly, or pork mince*
*2 tsp cornflour*
*pinch bicarbonate of soda*
*vegetable oil, for cooking*
*½ tsp finely diced ginger*
*1 clove garlic, finely diced*
*1 tbsp chilli bean sauce*
*1 tbsp yellow soybean paste*
*1 tbsp sweet bean paste*
*2 tbsp tomato ketchup*
*¼ tsp Chinkiang vinegar (optional)*
*150g fresh wonton noodles, or 125g dried noodles*

Visit any noodle shop in Hong Kong or Guangzhou and you will find *ow larm fun* on their menu. This dish has earned its classic status by offering meltingly tender beef brisket in a pool of dark velvety sauce, all atop soft rice noodles. Sichuan pepper is rarely used in Cantonese cooking but here it adds a background hum to the sauce. The sauce is also excellent for rice and we encourage you to double the recipe for freezing.

# star anise braised beef on rice noodles

1  If you are adding an exotic: soak the *ji jook* in a bowl of cold water for 30 minutes. Drain and discard the water, and cut the *ji jook* into 5cm long pieces.

2  Put the beef into a medium saucepan, pour in 700ml boiling water, cover and bring to the boil. Turn off the heat, remove the beef with a slotted spoon and drain in a bowl lined with kitchen paper. Pour the broth into a bowl and set aside.

3  Add the oil to the now empty pan and heat over a medium heat. Add the ginger and fry for 20 seconds, then add the garlic and fry for a further 20 seconds. Return the beef to the pan and fry until the edges are browned. Pour in the reserved broth. Add the rest of the ingredients, except the noodles and cornflour, and bring to the boil. Reduce the heat to low, cover and simmer for 30 minutes. Turn off the heat and allow the pan to sit on the hob for 30 minutes.

4  Bring the mixture back to the boil then reduce the heat and simmer for 1 hour. During the last 15 minutes, add the *ji jook*, if using, and simmer uncovered until the liquid has reduced.

5  Meanwhile, soak the rice noodles in a bowl of cold water for 30 minutes, then drain. Cook the noodles in a pan of boiling water according to the packet instructions until al dente.

6  In a small bowl, mix the cornflour and 2 tablespoons water into a slurry, then stir into the beef. Bring back to a bubble to cook the cornflour for 2 minutes. Serve divided between bowls.

**Serves 2–3**

*500g beef brisket, cut into 3 x 3cm cubes*
*1 tbsp vegetable oil*
*3 pieces ginger, each the size of a garlic clove, smashed*
*2 cloves garlic, smashed*
*2 tbsp hoisin sauce*
*2 tbsp oyster sauce*
*1 tsp dark soy sauce*
*1 tsp granulated sugar*
*large pinch salt*
*½ tsp Sichuan pepper*
*3 star anise*
*3 dried whole chillies*
*150g dried wide rice noodles*
*1 tbsp cornflour*

 **add an exotic (see page 14)**

*30g ji jook (dried beancurd)*

These glossy noodles are simply slurp-worthy as a quick snack. We find that the best noodles to use here is wholewheat spaghetti because the nutty flavour stands up well to the punchy hot and sour of the dressing. Try to choose a chilli oil that has lots of sediment – the chillies and other ingredients that the oil was soaked in – visible at the bottom of the jar.

# spicy and sour noodles

1 Bring a large saucepan of water to the boil and cook the spaghetti until al dente. Drain in a colander, rinse under cold water, then shake off any excess water.

2 Put the spaghetti in a bowl and mix in the rest of the ingredients, adjusting each to your own taste. Serve with some extra chilli oil, just in case you are in the mood for a more fiery kick.

**Serves 2, or one very hungry person**

*150g dried wholewheat spaghetti*

*1–2 tsp chilli oil, plus its sediment*

*1 tsp sesame oil*

*1½ tsp Chinkiang vinegar*

*½ tsp soft brown sugar*

*scant ¼ tsp salt*

*¼ spring onion, thinly sliced diagonally*

*1 small fresh red chilli, sliced*

Having noodles for breakfast is commonplace in China and growing up, we always craved Dad's version. To his fantastic recipe, we've added a sunny twist: a fried egg crowned with a halo of caramelised soy sauce – just because everything is better with a fried egg.

# breakfast noodles

1 Soak the noodles in a bowl of boiling water for 5 minutes until softened. Use a fork or pair of chopsticks to loosen the noodles every now and then.

2 Meanwhile, fry an egg to your liking. We like our yolks runny.

3 Carefully drain the water from the noodles, leaving about a tablespoon of cooking water in the bottom. Add the salt, pepper, sugar, sesame oil and 1 teaspoon soy sauce and mix to coat each strand in the seasonings.

4 When the egg is almost done, drizzle the remaining soy sauce around the egg. Let the sauce bubble furiously until it has all seeped into the edges of the egg. Serve the fried egg on top of the noodles.

**Serves 1**

*80g dried rice vermicelli noodles*

*1 large egg*

*vegetable oil, for frying*

*¼ tsp salt*

*¼ tsp ground white pepper*

*½ tsp granulated sugar*

*1 tsp sesame oil*

*2 tsp light soy sauce*

*1 tsp vegetable oil*

It's always exciting to chance upon new and unexpected ways of using old ingredients. There's no better example of this than turning egg noodles into crunchy fritters. As the sweet chilli in the batter sizzles in the hot oil, the sugar caramelises and turns the fritters a mouthwatering golden-brown colour. Serving the fritters with extra sweet chilli sauce makes for a brilliant zingy accompaniment – just be sure to have napkins nearby for those sticky fingers.

# sticky fingers noodle fritters

1 Cook the noodles in a pan of boiling water according to the packet instructions until al dente. Drain and set aside.

2 Lightly beat the eggs in a bowl. Sift the flour and baking powder into the eggs and whisk until smooth. Stir in the remaining ingredients, except for the oil, then add the noodles. Use a pair of chopsticks to separate out the noodles so that every strand is lightly coated in the batter.

3 In a large frying pan with high sides, pour in the oil to a depth of about 5mm and put the pan over a medium heat. To test if the oil is ready, drop a single noodle into the oil. It should sizzle instantly. Using a tablespoon and a fork, gently twist the noodles into bundles (making sure not to coil too tightly otherwise the fritters won't be delicate and crisp) and carefully slip the bundles into the hot oil. Use a fish slice to gently press down to flatten the fritters and shallow-fry for 1–2 minutes on each side, or until golden brown. Remove and drain on kitchen paper. Serve immediately with loads of sweet chilli sauce.

Makes 15–20
200g dried egg noodles
2 large eggs
4 tbsp plain flour
½ tsp baking powder
2 tbsp finely chopped fresh coriander
½ tsp freshly ground black pepper
½ tsp salt
3 tbsp sweet chilli sauce, plus extra to serve
vegetable oil, for shallow-frying

Let's face it, most food is better when it's *bok bok cheow* (super-crispy), but these deep-fried noodles are more than just a naughty treat: the architectural 'nest' acts as a lacy podium for the saucy topping to rest on. We have made a vegetarian version here but you could easily add some stir-fried meat (coat in cornflour before cooking) along with a dash of oyster sauce, if you like.

# crispy noodle nests

1   Cook the noodles in a pan of boiling water according to the packet instructions, then tip into a colander and shake off as much excess water as possible. Stir in a few drops of oil to stop the noodles from sticking to each other while they cool.

2   Pour enough vegetable oil into a large, deep saucepan to a depth of 4cm and put over a medium-high heat. If you are using a deep-fryer, set the temperature at 180°C/350°F. To test that the oil is ready, drop a small piece of noodle into the oil. It should float to the surface immediately and turn dark brown in about 20 seconds. When the oil is ready, hold half the noodles high above the oil then slowly feed them into the saucepan so they don't clump together. Use a pair of chopsticks or tongs to loosen up the strands and coax the bundle into a circular shape. Deep-fry until crisp and golden brown (you might need to flip halfway through), then remove and drain on kitchen paper. Repeat with the remaining noodles.

3   Whisk the sauce ingredients together in a bowl.

4   Heat 2 tablespoons oil in a wok or large frying pan over a high heat and stir-fry the ginger, garlic and spring onion whites until fragrant. Add the carrot and celery, sprinkle in the rice wine and stir-fry until the vegetables have softened slightly. Add the mushrooms, pak choi and spring onion greens and stir-fry to coat the vegetables in oil. Add the sauce, bring to a gentle boil then reduce the heat and simmer for 5 minutes, stirring occasionally until it has thickened slightly.

5   Put the noodle nests in shallow serving dishes and tumble the vegetables on top. At the table, use chopsticks to break up the nest so that all the noodles are coated in the sauce, and tuck in.

## Serves 2–3

*60g thin dried egg noodles*

*2 tbsp vegetable oil, plus extra for deep-frying*

*1 tsp finely diced ginger*

*2 cloves garlic, finely diced*

*2 spring onions, green parts sliced into lengths, white parts of 1 finely sliced*

*½ medium carrot, sliced*

*½ celery stick, diagonally sliced*

*½ tbsp Shaoxing rice wine*

*70g fresh oyster or button mushrooms*

*100g pak choi, roughly chopped*

## for the sauce

*250ml unsalted vegetable stock*

*1½ tsp light soy sauce*

*½ tsp dark soy sauce*

*¼ tsp salt*

*1 tsp granulated sugar*

*½ tbsp cornflour*

banquet

Nothing will make you *lou sai hou sou* (literally, 'mouth water') like the tantalising sights and smells of a vibrant Cantonese feast. Perhaps you are faced with a huge circular restaurant table, on top of which a lazy Susan threatens to stop spinning under the burgeoning weight of an impressive spread. Or maybe you are getting ready to tuck in home-buffet style with your extended family, like we frequently did in New Zealand. Either way, it's time to brace yourself and loosen your belt because the Cantonese banquet is, in a word, lush.

Cantonese banqueting dishes are the most famous and special ones, and also usually among the crispiest, stickiest and richest, too. Sometimes they can take more time and love to prepare than everyday meals such as those found in the Chineasy and Sharing Menu chapters. Even so, a banquet is certainly achievable at home, and it is so terrific to eat and 'wow' friends and family with that these dishes are worth every minute spent in the kitchen.

Pair these dishes with plain steamed rice or do as our dad always has: savour the banquet dishes at an unhurried pace while sipping on a fine whiskey or Chinese grain wine. If you can still muster up some energy after dinner, make it a real Cantonese banqueting affair by whipping out the microphones and indulging in a spot of off-key karaoke!

Nobody makes sweet and sour pork like Mr Zhang – and he knows it. Dad's favourite thing to do after cooking a fresh batch at the market is to taste the sauce with a plastic spork and cheekily exclaim 'Mmm, wonderful!' in front of all the customers. It works a treat too: sweet and sour is one of our all-time bestselling dishes.

# dad's sweet and sour pork

1   In a bowl, combine the pork, salt, cornflour, bicarbonate of soda, garlic from 1 clove, and 2 teaspoons water. Set aside to marinate for 1 hour.

2   Make the batter. In a bowl, whisk 250ml water with the flour, 1 teaspoon baking powder, bicarbonate of soda and salt and pepper until well combined. Cover and leave in a warm place for 45 minutes.

3   When the pork has marinated, bring a large pan of water to the boil. Add the pork and loosen with a fork. When the water returns to the boil, drain the pork in a colander and allow to air-dry.

4   Mix the sauce ingredients with 120ml water, stirring well to ensure that the cornflour is completely dissolved. Set aside.

5   Heat enough oil for deep-frying in a saucepan with high sides. If using a deep-fryer, set the temperature to 180°C/350°F. To test that the oil is ready, drop a pea-sized dollop of batter into the oil. It should turn a pale gold in 20 seconds. Stir the remaining ½ teaspoon of baking powder into the batter and mix in the pork pieces. Carefully drop each piece of batter-covered pork into the oil from a height of about 4cm from the surface of the oil and as soon as you release the pork, rub your fingers together to minimise long batter tails. Deep-fry until golden, then remove and drain.

6   Return the pork to the hot oil to fry a second time until the nuggets are golden brown – this will give you a really crispy batter. Remove and drain on kitchen paper.

**Serves 4**
*400g pork loin or shoulder, cut into 2cm cubes*
*large pinch salt*
*1 tsp cornflour*
*¼ tsp bicarbonate of soda*
*3 cloves garlic, finely diced*
*2 tbsp vegetable oil, plus extra for deep-frying*
*2 tsp finely diced ginger*
*100g canned pineapple chunks*

**for the batter**
*200g plain flour*
*1½ tsp baking powder*
*½ tsp bicarbonate of soda*
*large pinch salt and ground white pepper*

**for the sauce**
*5 tbsp white vinegar*
*1 tbsp Worcestershire sauce*
*4 tbsp tomato ketchup*
*5 tbsp granulated sugar*
*¼ tsp pinches salt*
*2 tsp cornflour*

7   For the sauce, heat 2 tablespoons oil over a medium heat and fry
    the ginger and the remaining garlic until aromatic. Pour in the sauce
    mixture and bring to a simmer, stirring constantly for 2–3 minutes
    until the sauce changes from opaque to translucent, and has
    thickened. Adjust the amount of sugar and vinegar to taste. Add the
    pork and pineapple, gently stir to coat, then serve.

Nothing says banquet like a succulent slab of pork belly encrusted in five-spice powder and topped with a delightfully light and crispy crackling. A few clever tricks from Mum will help you to achieve that *bok bok cheow* (super-crispy) crackling: prick the skin all over while it is hot out of the poaching liquid, and pat on a layer of salt to dry out the skin during roasting.

# mum's cracking five-spiced roast pork belly

1   Preheat the oven to 180°C/350°F/Gas mark 4. On the meaty side of the pork, make a series of parallel cuts about 2cm apart and to within 1cm of the skin. Place the pork, skin-side down, in a large stockpot and cover completely with boiling water. Use a heavy bowl to weigh the pork down if it starts to curl up and simmer gently for 10 minutes. Transfer the pork, skin-side up, to a plate and leave to cool slightly.

2   While the pork is still hot, hold 12 bamboo skewers as you would a fat pencil and prick the pork skin all over. Make sure to pierce right through to the fat layer. Flip over.

3   Combine the ingredients for the rub together in a small bowl and apply all over the meaty side of the pork, making sure to get into every crevice and avoiding the skin. Place the pork, skin side-up, on a wire rack set inside a roasting tray.

4   Use a long, sharp knife to scrape excess moisture away from the skin, and dab away with kitchen paper. Spread the 2 tablespoons of salt over the skin in an even layer and roast the pork for 40 minutes. Keep an eye on the skin and if any liquid pools on the surface, dab it away with kitchen paper.

5   Switch the oven to the grill setting and increase the temperature to 240°C/475°F/Gas mark 9. Peel off the layer of caked salt and dab the skin dry. Raise the pork so it is now 5cm from the grill element, keep the door ajar and grill for 10–15 minutes. If one area browns up faster than the rest, cover with foil. The pork is done when the skin forms layer upon layer of crackly bubbles. Cut into bite-size pieces, and serve.

**Serves 8-10**
*1kg slab belly pork, about 4cm thick, skin on*
*2 tbsp salt*

**for the rub**
*2 tsp five-spice powder*
*1 tbsp granulated sugar*
*2 tsp light soy sauce*
*1½ tsp salt*

*Suen houng gwut* are a mainstay of the Cantonese banqueting menu – a dish bursting with enough garlic to wipe out a whole colony of vampires. We've learnt that the secret to frying up the most sumptuous garlic rib is to marinate the meatiest rack you can find with plenty of garlic for a good few hours, then pack a dense crust around each individual rib. This way, they will be crispy on the outside, heavenly moist on the inside, and intensely garlicky all over.

# golden garlic ribs

1  Slice the rack into individual ribs and rinse them thoroughly in cold water. Shake off any excess water then transfer the ribs to a large bowl. Use your hands to massage the marinade ingredients into the ribs. Cover and leave to marinate in the fridge for at least 3 hours.

2  Before deep-frying the ribs, par-cook them in two batches to help them retain maximum juiciness. To steam, arrange the ribs on a steam-proof dish in a single layer and steam over vigorously boiling water for 5–6 minutes per batch. To microwave (in an 800w machine), arrange the ribs in a single layer, cover and cook for 4 minutes per batch.

3  Fill a large, deep saucepan two-thirds with oil and place over a medium-high heat. If you are using a deep-fryer, set the temperature to 180°C/350°F. Mix the cornflour and breadcrumbs together in a bowl, then use your hands to coat one rib at a time, packing the coating on as densely as you can. To test that the oil is ready, dip the handle of a wooden spoon into the oil. It should fizzle immediately, but the oil should not be smoking.

4  Carefully lower half the ribs into the hot oil and deep-fry for 1 minute, then drain and transfer to a wire rack with a baking tray set underneath. Repeat with the second batch. Return each batch to the hot oil to fry for a further 3–4 minutes, then drain and serve on a bed of shredded lettuce.

**Serves 4**

*1.2kg rack of pork ribs*
*vegetable oil, for deep-frying*
*handful shredded iceberg lettuce, to serve*

**for the marinade**
*12 cloves garlic, very finely diced*
*1 tsp Shaoxing rice wine.*
*1 tsp light soy sauce*
*1 tsp salt*
*¼ tsp ground white pepper*
*2 tsp cornflour*
*1 tsp bicarbonate of soda*

**for the coating**
*100g cornflour*
*60g fine breadcrumbs*

The Chinese characters for *char siu* literally mean 'fork' and 'roast', which reflect how the long, red strips are stabbed at one end with a hook and dangled inside a coal oven until their edges are deliciously charred. *Char siu* is easy to replicate at home and there are plenty of ways to enjoy it – serve as it is, use it to fill steamed and baked pork buns, or try it as a sandwich filling. For the glaze, maltose gives a high shine but doesn't have the floral sweetness of honey, so we like to use a bit of both.

# char siu pork

1   Mix all the marinade ingredients together in a large bowl, including the *narm yu*, if using. Add the pork to the marinade, and use your hands to massage it into the pork. Cover and chill overnight.

2   The next day, preheat the oven to 180°C/350°F/Gas mark 4. Line a baking tray with non-stick paper and set a wire rack on top. Arrange the pork on the rack, leaving at least 2cm between each strip. Keep the leftover marinade nearby. Roast the pork for 20 minutes, then brush with the leftover marinade, turn, brush the other side and roast for a further 20 minutes until the pork is cooked and a deep red colour, and the marinade has dried out.

3   Switch the oven setting to the grill setting. Mix the honey, maltose (if using) and 1 tablespoon boiling water together in a bowl. Remove the tray from the oven and brush the glaze over the pork. Return the tray to the top shelf and grill with the door slightly ajar for 2–3 minutes, until the edges char slightly, and there are tiny beads of glaze foaming on the surface. Turn and repeat for the other side.

4   Leave the pork to cool to room temperature and scrape the cooking juices into a bowl. Slice the pork into 3mm pieces to show off the crimson ring around the outer edge, fanning out the slices to emphasise the effect if you wish, and serve with the reserved cooking juices drizzled on top.

Serves 4–6
*800g pork neck, shoulder, or belly, sliced with the grain into 5cm-wide strips*

**for the marinade**
*½ tbsp honey*
*½ tbsp light soy sauce*
*1½ tbsp dark soy sauce*
*½ tbsp rice wine*
*1 tbsp hoisin sauce*
*1 tsp sesame oil*
*½ tsp ground white pepper*
*pinch five-spice powder (optional)*
*3 tbsp soft brown sugar*
*1 clove garlic, diced*
*½ tsp red food colouring (optional)*

**for the glaze**
*1 tbsp honey*
*1 tbsp maltose syrup (or use 2 tbsp honey)*
*½ tsp finely diced ginger*

 **add an exotic (see page 14)**
*½ cube of narm yu (red fermented beancurd)*

We always know when this dish is about to arrive at our restaurant table because the intense peppery aroma that wafts our way is always accompanied by the sound of the sauce bubbling on the scorching hotplate. If you want to re-create the restaurant experience at home you will find hotplates (often in the shape of an ox) in Chinese supermarkets, but a cast-iron frying pan will also do the trick. This recipe also works well with lamb.

# black peppercorn sizzling hotplate steak

1   Put the beef into a medium bowl, add the marinade ingredients and 4 tablespoons water and mix well. Cover and chill for at least 4 hours.

2   If you are using a sizzling hotplate, preheat the oven to 200°C/400°F/ Gas mark 6 and put the hotplate into the oven 30 minutes before you begin cooking.

3   Heat 1 tablespoon oil in a wok, or a large frying pan with high sides, over a high heat. Add the onion and stir-fry for 1 minute, or until softened. Add the green pepper and stir-fry for another minute. Sprinkle in 1 tablespoon water and stir-fry for 2 minutes until the peppers are cooked but still crunchy. Remove the onion and green pepper and set aside.

4   Reheat the wok over a high heat. Add the remaining 1½ tablespoons oil and the peppercorns and fry for 30 seconds. Add the ginger and garlic, fry until fragrant, then spread the marinated beef slices over the base of the wok in a single layer and brown for 1 minute. Flip every 30 seconds for a further 2 minutes or until the beef has a golden crust. Return the onion and green pepper to the wok, add the oyster sauce and toss to coat.

5   Reduce the heat to low. In a small bowl, mix the cornflour and 3 tablespoons water into a slurry then stir it into the wok. Increase the heat and toss everything for 1 minute, or until the sauce is translucent. If using, carefully remove the hotplate from the oven and spoon the beef onto the sizzling hot surface and serve.

**Serves 4**

*250g beef rump steak, cut against the grain into 3–5mm slices*
*2½ tbsp vegetable oil*
*½ onion, thickly sliced*
*1 green pepper, cut into 12 pieces*
*1 tbsp cracked black peppercorns*
*2 slices ginger, finely diced*
*1 clove garlic, finely diced*
*3 tbsp oyster sauce*
*½ tbsp cornflour*

**for the marinade**

*2 tsp finely diced ginger*
*pinch salt*
*½ tsp granulated sugar*
*½ tsp bicarbonate of soda*
*1½ tbsp cornflour*
*½ tbsp vegetable oil*
*1 tbsp Shaoxing rice wine*

The Chinese are an auspicious bunch and certain 'codes of practice' have been honed from centuries of chasing prosperity and good fortune. Finding opportunities to use the number eight, for example, is thought to encourage wealth because the Chinese word for eight (baht) rhymes with that of wealth (faht). Celebratory meals are the perfect time to make your own fortune and dishes like this one, with its eight star ingredients, are at the heart of such meals.

# eight treasures clay pot

1   Soak the Chinese mushrooms in 120ml hot water with a pinch of sugar for 30 minutes, then drain. Remove and discard the stalks and reserve the soaking liquid. Soak the snow fungus and vermicelli in separate bowls of cold water for 15 minutes, then drain. If adding an exotic: soak the *mook yee* in hot water for 30 minutes, then drain.

2   Heat 1 tablespoon vegetable oil in a 24cm clay pot or saucepan over the lowest heat and fry the ginger and garlic for a few minutes until fragrant. Pour in 250ml boiling water and the reserved Chinese mushroom soaking liquid, then add the Chinese mushrooms, deep-fried tofu, *mook yee* (if using), soy sauce, ½ teaspoon sugar and ¼ teaspoon salt. Cover and bring to a gentle boil, then reduce the heat and simmer for 20 minutes.

3   Meanwhile, for the garnish, slice the spring onion in half lengthways then cut it into 5cm lengths and put in a bowl of cold water to encourage them to curl up.

4   In a bowl, mix the cornflour and 3 tablespoons water into a slurry and set aside. Taste the liquid in the pan and season with salt to taste. Increase the heat to medium and nudge the drained vermicelli, shimeji mushrooms and snow fungus into the mix, then arrange the water spinach on top. Drizzle on the remaining ½ teaspoon vegetable oil, cover and simmer for 5 minutes. Reduce the heat to low, give the cornflour slurry a stir, then add it to the pan. Increase the heat and stir until the remaining liquid thickens slightly. Add the pepper, sesame oil and salt to taste. Garnish with the spring onion and serve.

**Serves 4**

4 dried Chinese mushrooms
granulated sugar
13g snow fungus
40g dried bean thread vermicelli
1 tbsp vegetable oil plus ½ tsp
2 large slices ginger, quartered and smashed
1 clove garlic, finely diced
4 pieces deep-fried tofu, sliced
1 tbsp light soy sauce
1 tsp cornflour
80g shimeji (clam shell) mushrooms, trimmed from the connective base
60g water spinach or any leafy green vegetable, cut into 5cm lengths
pinch ground white pepper
1 tsp sesame oil
salt
1 spring onion, to garnish

 **add an exotic (see page 14)**

4g mook yee (wood ear mushrooms)

*Bak chek gey* can be the centrepiece of a celebratory restaurant meal or a *sohng* (rice accompaniment) as part of an everyday family meal. The whole bird is tenderly poached and traditionally accompanied with a sauce of grated ginger and spring onions bathed in sizzling hot oil. For a quick and delicious meal the next day, try a simple soup of *bak chek gey* sauce, chicken stock and leftover steamed rice.

# poached chicken with ginger and spring onion sauce

1   Bring a large stockpot of water to the boil. There should be enough water to submerge the chicken with an extra 5cm to spare above. Turn the heat off once the water has boiled. Hold the chicken by its wing tips and dunk it breast-side down into the water, making sure that the cavity gets filled (watch for the bubbles to stop). Lift the chicken out and let all the water drain from the cavity. Repeat the dunk-and-lift twice more. Put the chicken on a plate and bring the water to the boil. Once again, turn off the heat and dunk-and-lift the chicken three times. Bring the water to a rapid boil. Turn off the heat and submerge the chicken. Cover and bring to the boil again over a low heat. As soon as the surface is burbling or murmuring, turn off the heat and leave the bird to sit in the water for 15 minutes.

2   Slowly bring the water to a burble again over a low heat. Turn off the heat and leave for another 10–15 minutes until the meat juices near the thickest part of the drumstick run clear when the tip of a sharp knife is inserted into it.

3   Make an ice bath by filling a large bowl with ice cubes and cold water. Carefully remove the chicken from the stockpot, being delicate with the skin, and submerge it in the ice bath. Turn the chicken every few minutes until it is completely chilled. Drain on kitchen paper, then rub the sesame oil all over the skin.

4   To make the sauce, heat the vegetable oil in a pan until sizzling hot and pour it over the rest of the sauce ingredients. Chop the chicken into chopstickable pieces and serve with the sauce.

**Serves 4**
*1.5kg good-quality whole chicken*
*ice cubes*
*½ tsp sesame oil*

**for the sauce**
*4 tbsp vegetable oil*
*3 tbsp finely grated ginger*
*2 spring onions, thinly sliced diagonally*
*½ tsp salt*
*pinch granulated sugar*

Whenever we have family over for big dinners at our house, we do it buffet style: the table is extended to its biggest possible surface area, then absolutely crammed to the perimeter with a vibrant array of dishes. Along with Dad's Sweet and Sour Pork (page 184), this super-*cheow* (crispy) and *gum* (golden) treat is always one of the first dishes to be polished off.

# lollipop chicken

1   The first step is to 'lollipop' the chicken. For the drumettes: hold on to the meaty end and use a sharp knife to carefully score the skin around the bone, just above the nobbly joint at the narrow end. Hold on to the nobbly joint with one hand and position the drumette at a 45° angle against the board. Insert the knife into the scored line and apply downward pressure to scrape the meat off the bone and towards the thicker end. Twist the bone around as you go to move the meat down to the bottom. Trim off any excess skin. For the flats: score the skin around the narrower end of the flat, then cut between the two bones to separate them. Hold one of the bones at a time and use the same method described above to scrape the meat towards the wider end of the flat, making sure to scrape between the two bones as well. Once all of the meat has moved to the bottom, remove one of the bones by holding it tightly, positioning the knife at the point where this bone is attached to the joint, and slicing through to release it.

2   Put the lollipops in a large bowl together with the marinade ingredients, then use your hands to massage the marinade into the chicken. Cover and chill for at least 30 minutes.

3   Fill a deep saucepan two-thirds with vegetable oil and put it over a medium-high heat. If you are using a deep-fryer, set the temperature to 180°C/350°F. To test if the oil is hot enough, mix a little cornflour with a little water and carefully drop it into the oil. It should fizz up, but not turn brown instantly. Mix the coating ingredients together in a large bowl. Working with one lollipop at a time, use your fingers to pat the coating generously all over the meat, avoiding the bone.

*(continues overleaf)*

**Serves 4**

*6 chicken wings, tips removed, separated into drumettes and flats (see tip overleaf)*
*vegetable oil, for deep-frying*
*salt, for sprinkling*

**for the marinade**
*½ tsp salt*
*¼ tsp light soy sauce*
*2 pinches ground white pepper*
*2 cloves garlic*

**for the coating**
*80g cornflour*
*¼ tsp chilli powder*
*pinch salt*
*2 pinches white pepper*

**for the dry-fry seasonings**
*2 tsp vegetable oil*
*2 cloves garlic, finely chopped*
*1 tsp crushed Sichuan peppercorns or 1 tsp cracked black pepper*
*3 spring onions, sliced*
*1 fresh red chilli, deseeded and thinly sliced*
*¼ tsp salt*

Deep-fry the chicken in batches for 1 minute before transferring them to a wire rack. Return each batch to the oil for a further 3–4 minutes until they are golden brown and crisp. Drain on the wire rack for a few minutes.

4    Meanwhile, cook the dry-fry seasonings. Heat 2 teaspoons vegetable oil in a wok over medium heat, add the dry-fry seasonings and fry for about 15 seconds until fragrant. Add the fried lollipops then stir-fry quickly for a minute to coat the chicken with the seasoned oil (don't worry if the bits don't stick to the chicken). To serve, sprinkle extra salt on top.

DUMPLING SISTERS TIP
The 'drumette' is the first section of the chicken wing between the shoulder and elbow while the 'flat' is the section between the elbow and the tip.

We wanted to include this fun dish as a homage to our Hakka roots from Dad's side of the family. The Hakka people have a reputation for being hardworking, which is what this recipe will ask of you, but the impressive end result is totally worth it.

# crispy duck stuffed with sticky rice

1 Wash and soak the rice in a bowl of cold water overnight.

2 The next day, prepare the duck legs. Starting at the thigh end, use the tip of a very sharp knife to carefully slice through the membrane-like tissue that connects the skin to the meat. Peel the skin away from the meat as you do so. Keep going until you reach the end of the drumstick, then use a cleaver to chop through the bone so that the tip of the drumstick is still attached to the skin, while the rest of the bone stays inside the meat. Turn the skin so it is right-side out again and resembles a deflated duck leg shape. Set aside.

3 Soak the Chinese mushrooms in a bowl of hot water with a pinch of sugar for 30 minutes, then drain. Remove and discard the stalks and dice the caps. If adding an exotic: soak the *har mey* in a bowl of hot water for 30 minutes, then drain.

4 Cut the duck meat from the bone, weigh out 120g for this dish, and store the rest for another meal. Cut the duck into 2 x 1cm pieces. Transfer to a bowl and mix in ¼ teaspoon salt, the light soy sauce, ½ teaspoon sugar and the cornflour. Leave to marinate for at least 20 minutes.

5 Heat the oil in a wok or frying pan over a high heat and briefly stir-fry the ginger and Sichuan pepper until fragrant. Add the garlic and pork belly and stir-fry for a few minutes to render the oil out of the pork. Add the marinated duck and stir-fry for a few more minutes until cooked. Leave to cool slightly.

6 Drain the rice and add it to the cooked meat together with the diced mushrooms, spring onions, and *har mey*, if using. Add the remaining ¼ teaspoon salt and 2 tablespoons water and mix to combine.

**Serves 4–6**

*100g glutinous rice*
*4 large duck legs (1.2kg total)*
*3 dried Chinese mushrooms*
*granulated sugar*
*½ tsp salt*
*1 tsp light soy sauce*
*2 tsp cornflour*
*1 tbsp vegetable oil, plus extra for oiling*
*2 tsp finely diced ginger*
*¼ tsp ground Sichuan pepper*
*2 cloves garlic, finely diced*
*50g pork belly, finely diced*
*2 spring onions, thinly sliced*
*1 tsp dark soy sauce*

 **add an exotic (see page 14)**
*1 tbsp har mey (dried shrimp)*

7   Loosely pack each of the skins with a quarter of the rice filling and arrange on a lightly oiled steam-proof plate.

8   Steam over a medium boil for 40 minutes until the rice is cooked through, topping up the pan with extra hot water as needed. Meanwhile, preheat the oven to 200°C/400°F/Gas mark 6 and line a baking sheet with non-stick paper.

9   Remove the duck from the steamer and leave to cool for 10 minutes. Carefully transfer to the prepared baking sheet and rub 2 drops of dark soy sauce evenly over each leg then bake for 10 minutes until the skin is crisp and golden brown. Slice and serve.

This dish puts the ethos of Cantonese cooking on show with its simple balance of flavours between the fresh crab and ubiquitous ginger and spring onion. Ask your fishmonger for female crabs ('hens', wider abdomen flap) as they offer more richly flavoured brown meat than the males ('cocks'), along with decadent crab roe. During cooking the brown meat and roe melt into the *bao*'d (literally 'exploded') ginger and spring onions. This melty mixture both sauces the crab and serves as a wondrous dressing for the noodles underneath.

# spring onion, ginger and garlic crab

1   Heat 3 tablespoons oil in a wok or large saucepan over a medium-high heat and stir-fry or *bao* (explode) the ginger, spring onion whites and half the chilli until fragrant.

2   Meanwhile, in a large bowl, mix ½ teaspoon cornflour and ½ tablespoon water into a slurry, then add the crab (except for the lids) and toss to coat. Add the crab to the wok and turn several times to coat them in the oil. Place the crab lids on top, inside facing up. Sprinkle in 3 tablespoons water and cover to trap in the smoky *wok hei* (breath of the wok). Reduce the heat to medium and cook for 2 minutes, before stirring in a further 3 tablespoons water and 1 tablespoon oil. Cover and cook for a further 5–6 minutes, stirring halfway through.

3   Meanwhile, cook the noodles in a pan of boiling water according to the packet instructions, then drain and coat with a few drops of oil.

4   Reduce the heat to low under the wok then, in a bowl, mix the remaining cornflour and 60ml water into a slurry and pour it into the wok. Increase the heat and simmer, stirring regularly until the sauce has thickened. Reduce the heat and add the spring onion greens, the rest of the chilli, the pepper, sugar and ¼ teaspoon salt and mix well to combine. Drizzle in the remaining oil and mix to evenly coat everything until glossy. Serve piping hot on top of the noodles.

**Serves 4–6**

*6 tbsp vegetable oil*

*2 tbsp finely diced ginger*

*6 spring onions, cut into lengths, white parts lightly smashed*

*2 fresh red chillies, thinly sliced*

*1½ tsp cornflour*

*2 large fresh brown crab (about 1.3kg total), cleaned and prepared, lids kept, divided into quarters*

*150g dried egg noodles*

*6 spring onions, green parts only, cut into 5cm long pieces*

*pinch ground white pepper*

*¼ tsp granulated sugar*

*¼ tsp salt*

For us, fresh whole prawns are best eaten in one of two ways: simply blanched, so you can enjoy their natural sweetness (see page 104), or intoxicated with flavour. This recipe is a fantastic example of the latter with its brazen use of garlic and char-kissed shells. You could also do this with peeled prawns, but we think it's more of a fun challenge to unpeel them with just chopsticks and teeth . . . after you've unabashedly sucked off all the garlicky crust, that is.

# garlic-crusted king prawns

1  Use a small knife to cut down the back of each prawn to half its thickness. Pat the prawns dry on kitchen paper and rub in the salt.

2  In a small bowl, mix the cornflour and ½ teaspoon water into a slurry and set aside.

3  Heat 2 tablespoons oil in a wok or a large pan over a medium heat and stir-fry the garlic for about 30 seconds until the oil is fragrant and the garlic is just starting to brown. Immediately take the wok off the heat and scoop the garlic into a bowl, leaving any extra oil in the wok.

4  Pour the cornflour slurry over the salted prawns, toss to coat. Reheat the wok over a high heat until it is smoking hot and add 2 tablespoons oil. Put the prawns in the wok in a single layer and fry undisturbed for 1 minute. Flip each prawn over, drizzle in the remaining 1 tablespoon oil and sear for another 30 seconds, then quickly stir-fry until the flesh loses its transparency. Return the garlic to the wok and toss to coat the prawns before serving.

**Serves 4**

*400g raw king prawns, heads removed and deveined*
*¼ tsp salt*
*¼ tsp cornflour*
*5 tbsp vegetable oil*
*5 cloves garlic, finely diced*

# chinese bakery

Walk through any Chinatown, in any city, and you will know at once if the ovens of a Hong Kong-style bakery are blazing away long before you arrive at the inviting facade of the shop front. The giveaway? An irresistible aroma that perfumes the air; a warm, sweet scent that diffuses through the streets like a silent snake-charming song, luring us towards light and fluffy breads, pillow-soft cakes, rich pastries and gorgeously crumbly biscuits that just can't be reconciled with the word 'diet'.

In the West, Cantonese food is not typically associated with baking, and yet it is a much-loved part of the cuisine. In Hong Kong the fanciest bakeries dress their windows with mind-boggling cakes, often shaped into uncanny likenesses of Hello Kitty and fresh fruit. But our favourite bakery in London's Chinatown forgoes these elaborate displays. Their self-service layout is welcoming: patrons simply pick up a plastic tray and a pair of tongs at the front door, before shuffling through the store to make their selections from clear plastic-fronted cabinets that look like they have been cobbled together by someone's dad. It feels as if the entire store is sheathed in a soft glow, an effect of the perfectly golden and glazed tops of fresh buns and cakes.

Sounds lovely, so what could be better? Re-creating the baked heaven in your own home. It is with great pride and enthusiasm that we share our recipes for homemade Chinese baked goods. Whether you are after tasty afternoon tea treats or something with celebratory flair, simply flip through this chapter and you will discover something that may be pleasantly surprising: there's absolutely nothing half-baked about a Chinese bakery.

We have been eating a packaged version of these our whole lives, but it wasn't until we were guests at a Singaporean family's Chinese New Year celebration that we experienced the unbeatable moreishness of the homemade version. With pastry so *faa* that it instantly melts in your mouth, and jam that is satisfyingly chewy, we guarantee you'll be hooked after your first bite.

# pineapple tarts

1   First prepare the filling. Use your hands to squeeze as much liquid from the pineapple as you can, then blitz the squeezed pineapple in a food processor until the largest pieces are roughly the size of pine nuts. Transfer to a small saucepan and add the sugar, cloves, and salt. Cook over a low heat, stirring occasionally for 40–50 minutes until most of the moisture has evaporated. The pineapple should be a deep yellow colour. Leave to cool.

2   For the dough, put the flours, icing sugar, and salt into a large bowl. Working as quickly as you can, use your fingertips to rub the butter and lard into the dry ingredients until the majority of the mixture resembles fine crumbs. Mix in the egg yolk and vanilla. Squeeze lightly to bring the mixture together and form into a rough ball. Cover tightly with cling film and chill for 30 minutes until firm.

3   Preheat the oven to 180°C/350°F/Gas mark 4 and line a baking sheet with non-stick paper.

4   To form the tarts, divide the filling into 20 almond-sized pieces and with lightly oiled hands, shape each piece into a fat cylinder. Take a heaped ½ tablespoon of dough and flatten into a 5cm disc. Create a dip in the centre and add a piece of filling then wrap the dough around the filling. It should look like a fat sausage. Applying the lightest pressure, roll the sausage back and forth in your palm until the outside is smooth.

5   In a bowl, whisk the egg yolk with 1 teaspoon water and brush this mixture onto each tart. Use small scissors to make rows of V-shaped snips on the surface and chill for 20 minutes. Bake for 15–18 minutes until golden yellow. Leave to cool completely on a wire rack. Store in an airtight container for up to one week.

**Serves 4**

*432g canned pineapple chunks, drained*
*45g granulated sugar*
*10 cloves*
*pinch salt*
*1 egg yolk, for glazing*

**for the dough**

*175g plain flour*
*25g cornflour*
*75g icing sugar*
*pinch salt*
*100g cold unsalted butter, cubed*
*25g cold lard or vegetable shortening, cubed*
*1 egg yolk*
*¼ tsp vanilla extract*
*vegetable oil, for greasing*

The simple and literal name of these cakes belies a wonderfully light and eggy cake with a beautiful golden crust. Although it looks like a sponge from the outside, the texture inside is quite unique: the crumb is very fine with a slightly *daan* (springy) bite quality. We like to bake ours in a muffin tin for a pretty mini version, before loading them up with a lychee cream for extra sweetness and texture.

# paper-wrapped cakes

1   Preheat the oven to 170°C/340°F/Gas mark 3. Prepare your muffin tin by lining the holes with squares of non-stick paper.

2   Put all the ingredients for the yolk mixture, except the flour, into a large bowl, and use a hand whisk to whisk until the yolks are slightly pale in colour. Sift in the flour and whisk again until smooth. The batter will be very thick at this stage.

3   For the meringue, beat the egg whites in a large, clean, grease-free bowl until they become frothy, then gradually add the sifted icing sugar and continue beating until the whites are opaque and glossy, and stiff peaks form.

4   Add a third of the egg whites to the yolk batter and use a whisk to gently combine the two. Repeat with the remaining egg whites, folding them in gently until they have just combined with the mixture. Pour or spoon the cake mixture into the prepared cups until they are two-thirds full and bake for 20–25 minutes, or until the cakes are golden brown. Turn the oven off and open the door, leaving the cakes inside for a further 5 minutes. Then pop the tray on top of a wire rack and leave the cakes to cool completely before twisting them out of the cups.

5   In a bowl, whip the cream to soft peaks and stir in the sifted icing sugar followed by the chopped lychees and lychee juice (or liqueur). Spoon the cream generously on top of the cakes to serve.

**Makes 12 muffin-sized cakes**
**for the yolk mixture**
*3 egg yolks*
*1 whole egg*
*½ tsp vanilla extract*
*55ml vegetable oil*
*70g self-raising flour*

**for the meringue**
*3 egg whites*
*65g icing sugar, sifted*

**for the lychee cream**
*200ml double cream*
*3 tbsp icing sugar, sifted*
*100g canned lychees, roughly chopped*
*1 tsp lychee juice from the can or 1 tsp lychee liqueur*

If you have ever been inside a Chinese supermarket around Chinese New Year, you may have noticed the red-lidded containers stacked to the brim with little golden-brown cookies. *Hup toh soh*, or walnut cookies, are frequently gifted around this time. Walnuts are thought to symbolise the happiness of the entire family and their physical resemblance to a brain is supposed to boost mental prowess. Using lard makes for a supremely crumbly texture, but they are still delicious if you wish to use vegetable shortening instead.

# sweet and salty walnut cookies

1   Preheat the oven to 170°C/340°F/Gas mark 3½ and line a baking sheet with non-stick paper. Mix the flours, salt and bicarbonate of soda together in a large bowl. Sift twice between two different bowls in order to fully incorporate the flours. In another bowl, use a wooden spoon to beat the butter and lard together until they are thoroughly combined. Beat in the sugar, vanilla and 2 teaspoons of the beaten egg. Sift the flour mixture into the wet ingredients along with the walnuts, then fold and mix until it is a smooth ball of dough.

2   Roll ½ tablespoons of the cookie dough into compact balls and arrange them on the prepared baking sheet, making sure that there is at least 3cm of space between each cookie. Use a small bottle cap to slightly flatten each ball. You should be able to see an impression of a circle on the surface. Brush the remaining beaten egg over the tops and sides of the cookies and bake for 15–20 minutes until the cookies are golden brown.

3   Leave the cookies to cool completely on a wire rack before serving with a cup of tea or crumbling over vanilla ice cream. Store in an airtight container where it will keep for up to one week.

**Makes 40–50**
*190g plain flour*
*65g cornflour*
*¼ tsp salt*
*½ tsp bicarbonate of soda*
*75g unsalted butter, softened*
*75g lard or vegetable shortening (see tip), softened*
*110g granulated sugar*
*½ tsp vanilla extract*
*1 egg, beaten*
*10 walnut halves, finely chopped*

DUMPLING SISTERS TIP
If using vegetable shortening instead of lard, switch off the oven after baking but leave the cookies inside for a further 2–3 minutes so they have a chance to dry out – this will give you an airier texture.

From Tiger Cake to Pineapple Tarts, you could say that the Chinese enjoy making edible art that imitates life. *Bo lo bao* are no exception, and even though there's no pineapple, the name describes a streusel-like top that looks like a tasty approximation of the tropical fruit itself. Sink your teeth into one and you will love the duo of mouthfeels: the *soung* (crumbly) layer of the pineapple topping and the *meen* (bouncy, cottony soft) body of the bun.

# pineapple buns

1  Line a baking sheet with non-stick paper. Divide the sweet bread dough into 10 portions of about 70g each and shape into domes. Place onto the prepared baking sheet, cover with cling film then a tea towel and leave to rest in a warm place for 1–1½ hours until doubled in size.

2  Meanwhile, combine the dry ingredients for the topping in a bowl. Beat in the egg yolks, butter and 1 teaspoon water until evenly combined into a buttery dough. Shape into a fat sausage, wrap in cling film and chill for at least 20 minutes until firm.

3  Preheat the oven to 180°C/350°F/Gas mark 4. Divide the dough for the topping into 10 equal-sized pieces, then roll each out to a 2mm-thick disc – this is easiest done between two sheets of cling film. Lay a disc on top of each bun – gently moulding it into a dome shape – and brush with egg wash. Use the tip of a bamboo skewer to score a cross-hatch pattern into the topping dough.

4  Bake for 10–12 minutes until sunshine yellow. These are best eaten warm, or store in an airtight container for up to three days.

**Makes 10**

*1 batch of sweet bread dough, up to first rise (end of step 3, page 44)*

*1 egg, beaten*

**for the topping**

*110g plain flour*
*80g granulated sugar*
*¼ tsp bicarbonate of soda*
*¼ tsp baking powder*
*2 tbsp custard powder*
*2 egg yolks*
*60g unsalted butter, softened*

It was during a family trip to Guangzhou back in 2003 that we first set eyes on this fabulous creation, rather sweetly named tiger cake because of its evocative stripy 'skin', which is made by baking a cornflour mixture at a high temperature. To this day the best tiger cake we have ever eaten was from the hole-in-the-wall bakery near our grandmother's house, but we think that this one comes close.

# tiger cake

1   Preheat the oven to 180°C/350°F/Gas mark 4 and line a Swiss roll tin with non-stick paper. For the inner cake, beat the egg whites in a large, clean, grease-free bowl and gradually add 60g of the sugar until soft peaks form. Set aside.

2   Beat the egg yolks and the remaining 20g sugar in another bowl for 2 minutes, until they have thickened slightly and become a pale yellow colour. Beat for another minute, gradually adding the oil. Add the vanilla, food colouring and milk, then beat for 1 minute.

3   Mix the flours and baking powder together in a bowl. Sift the flour mixture twice between two different bowls. Sift the flour mixture again into the beaten egg yolk mixture, and whisk until smooth. Use a spatula to gently fold in half of the beaten egg whites into the yolk mixture. Repeat with the remaining egg whites, folding only until just combined.

4   Pour the mixture into the prepared tin and smooth over the top. Make sure that the mixture is spread out to the edges of the tin. Bake for 15 minutes until golden brown.

5   Meanwhile, prepare the tiger skin. Beat the egg yolks, sugar and vanilla in a large bowl until thick and pale. Add the cornflour and beat until smooth. Set aside.

6   Lift the cooked inner cake out of the tin by the paper and place onto a wire rack. Increase the oven temperature to 240°C/475°F/Gas mark 9. Leave the inner cake to cool for 3 minutes, then cut a 1cm-wide

*(continues overleaf)*

**Makes 1**

**for the inner cake**
*4 eggs, separated*
*80g granulated sugar*
*3 tbsp vegetable oil*
*4 drops vanilla extract*
*2 drops red food colouring*
*50ml full-fat milk*
*60g plain flour*
*20g cornflour*
*½ tsp baking powder*

**for the tiger skin**
*6 egg yolks*
*60g caster sugar*
*¼ tsp vanilla extract*
*20g cornflour*

**for the filling**
*150ml double cream,*
 *whipped*
*1½ tbsp icing sugar*

strip off one of the short sides. Gently score a line 1cm in from the cut edge of the cake, slicing down about halfway into the depth of the cake, then roll the whole thing – the cake and paper – into a firm spiral before putting it onto a wire rack.

7   Line the tin with a new sheet of non-stick paper, pour in the tiger skin mixture, and smooth over the top. Make sure that the mixture is spread out to the edges of the tin. Bake in the oven for 2–3 minutes. As soon as you can make out a stripy pattern, remove from the oven immediately. Lift the tiger skin out of the tin by the paper and put it on the wire rack. Leave to cool for 5 minutes, then carefully peel the skin away from the paper.

8   To roll your tiger cake, take a piece of non-stick paper that is a little larger than the cake. Put the tiger skin on the paper, pattern side down, then unroll the inner cake on top of the tiger skin and line it up at the edge that is closest to you. The tiger skin should be slightly longer than the inner cake on the far side. Spread the whipped cream on top of the inner cake, then use the paper to help you firmly roll the tiger cake. Twist the sides of the paper so the cake looks like a wrapped lolly and leave until ready to serve with tea (a Chinese green tea called *bi luo chun*, or 'spring snail' is an excellent choice).

The cute domes of these pastries belie the sophisticated layers nesting within. Like Custard Egg Tarts (page 232) the pastry layers are achieved by alternating layers of water dough and butter dough.

# flaky red bean pastries

1 Make the butter dough. In a large bowl, mix the flours together. Use your fingertips to rub in the butter then use the heel of one hand to fold and press the dough until the butter is evenly incorporated. Shape into a ball, wrap in cling film and chill for 30 minutes.

2 Make the water dough. In a large bowl, stir together the flours, sugar and 75ml cold water. Turn out onto a work surface, dot the butter all over the dough and using the heel of your hand, coax the butter into the dough until just evenly combined. Wrap in cling film and chill for 20 minutes.

3 For both doughs, divide into 15 portions and then form each portion into a ball. Use a damp cloth to cover the dough pieces that you are not working on to prevent them from drying out.

4 Take a portion of water dough and flatten into a disc. Place a ball of butter dough in the centre. Ease the water dough up and around the butter dough and pinch firmly at the top to create an even seal. Put the ball back under the damp cloth. Repeat with the remaining dough and leave to rest for 10 minutes.

5 Retrieve the first ball of dough that you worked with and put a rolling pin directly on top. Roll upward in one motion, then return the pin to where you started and roll down in another motion. You should end up with a stretched out oval shape, about 6cm wide and 12cm long. Lift the bottom edge and roll the pastry up into a scroll shape. Put back under the damp cloth. Repeat with the remaining dough, and leave to rest for 10 minutes.

*(continues overleaf)*

**Makes 15**
*1 egg yolk, beaten, for brushing*

**for the butter dough**
*125g plain flour*
*45g cornflour*
*85g unsalted butter, at room temperature and cubed*

**for the water dough**
*50g strong bread flour*
*90g plain flour*
*30g cornflour*
*40g icing sugar*
*50g unsalted butter, at room temperature and cubed*

**for the filling**
*175g sweet red bean paste*

6   Put a scroll in front of you with the seal running vertically. Using the same upward then downward rolling motion as before, roll the dough into a stretched-out oval, about 4cm wide and 12cm long. Roll into a scroll as before, repeat with the remaining dough, and leave to rest under the damp cloth for 10 minutes.

7   Preheat the oven to 180°C/350°F/Gas mark 4 and line a baking sheet with non-stick paper. Using oiled hands, roll the red bean paste into heaped ½ tablespoon-sized balls. If the red bean paste is too soft to handle, place it in the freezer for 30 minutes to firm up.

8   Put a scroll in your hand with the seal facing upward. Use your thumb to pinch down in the middle so that the scroll folds in half. Put the dough smooth side facing down on the work surface, flatten with your palm and then roll it out into an 8cm disc. Put a ball of red bean paste into the centre of the disc and wrap the dough up and around the filling and pinch to seal tightly at the top. Turn the filled dough over and place sealed-side down onto the prepared baking sheet and repeat with the remaining dough, leaving at least 3cm between each ball of dough.

9   Brush the egg yolk over the pastries and bake for 25 minutes until golden brown. Cool on a wire rack. These will keep in an airtight container for up to a week.

This colourful twist on fluffy chiffon cake originated in South-east Asia and has long been a Chinese bakery favourite. Traditionally, the cake mixture is dyed bright green by adding juice squeezed from the leaves of the pandan (*pandanus amaryllifolius*) plant. Luckily for those of us in short supply of pandan leaves, the extract is available in Chinese supermarkets and online (see page 265).

# mum and dad's vibrant pandan cake

1 Preheat the oven to 170°C/340°F/Gas mark 3 and grease a 24cm ring cake tin with oil. Mix together the flours, then sift the mixture twice between two different bowls to combine the flours evenly. Put the egg yolks into a large bowl and use an electric whisk to beat the yolks for 2 minutes until they are thick and pale. Add the 1½ tablespoons sugar, the milk, pandan essence, and 1½ tablespoons oil and beat for a further 3 minutes, gradually adding the remaining 3 tablespoons oil until thick and glossy. Add the baking powder and salt and beat for another 30 seconds to combine. Sift the flour mixture into the egg yolk mixture and beat until the mixture is smooth. Set aside.

2 Put the egg whites and lemon juice into a large, clean, grease-free bowl and use an electric beater to beat the egg whites for 1 minute until light and fluffy. Gradually add the 80g sugar as you beat the egg whites for a further 5 minutes, until glossy and stiff peaks form.

3 Use a whisk to gently fold a third of the egg whites into the egg yolk mixture, then fold in the second third of the egg whites. Repeat with the last third of egg whites, until just combined, then pour the cake mixture into the prepared cake tin and smooth over the top. Bake for 20–25 minutes, or until a skewer inserted into the cake comes out clean. Remove the cake from the oven and put the cake, still in the tin, upside down on a wire rack to cool for 1 hour. Run a knife around the inside edge of the tin, transfer the cake to a wire rack and allow to cool completely. Serve generous slices with whipped cream or a cup of green tea (or both).

**Serves 6-8**

*20g cornflour*
*55g plain flour*
*4 large eggs, separated*
*1½ tbsp caster sugar, plus 80g for the egg whites*
*2 tbsp full-fat milk*
*¼ tsp pandan essence*
*4½ tbsp vegetable oil, plus extra for greasing*
*¾ tsp baking powder*
*¼ tsp salt*
*¼ tbsp lemon juice*
*whipped cream, to serve*

When we were younger, *dan tat* were Julie's absolute favourite dim sum with their irresistibly *waat* (silky smooth) custard and gazillion layers of *soung* (loose and crumbly) pastry. During a family trip to Guangzhou we had *yum cha* at the same restaurant every day, but on one occasion the *dan tat* had been taken off the menu. Not one to be deterred by 'staff only' entrances, our beloved and larger than life *gou yeh poh* (ninth great aunt) took little Julie by the hand and marched into the kitchen to demand answers . . . needless to say, 15 minutes later the dim sum carts were all sunny yellow with the unmistakable smell of freshly baked tarts wafting through the air.

# custard egg tarts

1  For the butter dough, use a fork or pastry cutter to cut the butter into the flour until evenly distributed, then repeat with the lard until you have a paste. Put the paste into the centre of a piece of cling film and fold into an 18 x 18cm square. Squeeze the dough into the corners of the square until it takes on the shape, and flatten evenly with your palms. The slab should be about 0.5cm thick. Chill for 30 minutes.

2  For the water dough, put the flour, beaten egg, sugar, salt and lard into a medium bowl. Add 40ml cold water and stir until it forms a dough. Turn out onto a lightly floured work surface and use the heels of your palms to bring the mixture together, kneading lightly until the ingredients are evenly distributed. Wrap the dough in cling film and chill for 30 minutes.

3  Meanwhile, prepare the filling. Gently heat the milk, sugar and vanilla in a small saucepan for 5–8 minutes until the sugar has melted, then leave to cool. Stir the beaten eggs into the cooled milk mixture and strain through a sieve twice. Set aside.

4  Roll the water dough out onto a lightly floured surface into a 20 x 40cm rectangle. Place the flattened square of butter dough into the centre of the rectangle. Fold in the overhanging flaps of water dough to wrap around the butter dough. Roll into a 20 x 40cm rectangle. Fold in half to form a square, then in half again to form a rough 10 x 20cm rectangle. Chill in the fridge for 20 minutes.

**Makes 14**

**for the butter dough**
*80g cold unsalted butter*
*100g plain flour*
*120g cold lard or vegetable shortening*

**for the water dough**
*125g plain flour, plus extra for dusting*
*¼ egg (about 15g), beaten*
*1 tbsp granulated sugar*
*¼ tsp salt*
*7g cold lard or vegetable shortening*

**for the filling**
*120ml full-fat milk*
*40g granulated sugar*
*¼ tsp vanilla extract*
*1 egg*

**5** Roll the chilled dough into a 20 x 40cm rectangle, fold into thirds, chill for 20 minutes, then repeat the folding and chilling once more.

**6** Preheat the oven to 160°C/325°F/Gas mark 3. Roll the chilled dough into a 20 x 30cm rectangle, then use a 9cm cookie cutter to cut out 14 pastry rounds and ease each into a 7cm tart case, or a muffin tray. Prick the bottom of each with a fork and arrange the tart cases on a baking sheet. Chill for 10 minutes.

**7** Remove the tart cases from the fridge and pour in the custard filling to just below half full. Bake for 13–15 minutes until the pastry is light golden and the custard puffs up slightly. Leave to cool in the cases for 10 minutes, then turn out onto a wire rack. Best served warm on the day they are made.

sweet tooth

As Kiwi kids growing up in a Chinese household it's not surprising that both cultures influenced the way we like to eat. This is true of the evening meal: shared savoury dishes served with rice, followed by a wedge of pavlova or bowl of ice cream. In fact, we ate mountains of ice cream so Dad could collect the 2-litre containers for use as 'Tupperware' at the market. Years later the ice cream has long melted into our hips, but the tall stacks of ice cream containers remain (at last count, 78 of them).

Although the idea of a dessert course is not commonplace in Chinese eating culture, it doesn't mean that sweet treats don't exist. Many of the recipes in the Chinese Bakery chapter are fantastic ways to finish off a meal. Fancy a slice of pandan cake with a dollop of cream? We say, 'yes please!'. In Hong Kong, speciality dessert restaurants sell a bedazzling variety of puddings at all times of the day. We think it's time to commandeer such delights for everyday eating.

The sweet treats in this chapter range from the very traditional (Glutinous Rice Dessert Dumplings) to the cheeky (Deep-fried Ice Cream). And, as tribute to the culture that nursed our sweet tooths, you will also find a few East-meets-West creations.

Brittle is an old-school kind of sweet treat: quite simply, sugar that has been caramelised with some tasty morsels suspended within. The classic Chinese version, *fah sung zjie ma tong*, is a clear golden amber confection with two *houng* (fragrant) ingredients: roasted peanuts and freshly toasted sesame seeds. For a surprising yet delightful kick we've added dried chilli flakes.

# peanut and sesame brittle

**Makes about 200g**

*15g sesame seeds*
*60g roasted salted peanuts*
*¼ tsp dried chilli flakes (optional)*
*150g granulated sugar*
*1½ tsp white vinegar*

1 Toast the sesame seeds in a small frying pan over a low heat for 5 minutes, or until they smell slightly smoky and nutty. Line a 20cm square baking tin with non-stick paper and set aside.

2 Sprinkle the peanuts, toasted sesame seeds and chilli flakes (if using) evenly over the lined tin.

3 Heat the sugar and vinegar in a small saucepan over a low heat, stirring gently until the sugar melts. Increase the heat to medium and bring the syrup to the boil. (Once boiling, avoid the temptation to stir the mixture.) Cover with a lid and boil for a further 7–8 minutes or until the syrup is a light amber colour.

4 Remove from the heat and immediately pour the syrup onto the nuts and seeds in the tin. Leave to cool for 3–4 minutes in the tin before lifting it out with the paper onto a chopping board. Chop the brittle into shards and leave to harden for a further 40 minutes before munching. Store in an airtight container, where it will keep for at least a week.

DUMPLING SISTERS TIP
For maximum dramatic flair, you can wait for the brittle to cool completely before using a small hammer to crack it into irregular shards.

Fabulous alliteration aside, these gorgeous puddings really do live up to their name. If you have ever tried the Chinese restaurant variety you may have been disappointed by its somewhat processed quality: overly jellified and artificially mango-ey. Our homemade version blows the 'just add water' ones out of the, err . . . water. With an inviting warm yellow hue and a hint of richness afforded by a coconut milk base, this refreshing pudding is the ideal way to finish off a summer meal.

# marvellous mango pud

1   In a small bowl, soak the gelatine powder in 60ml cold water for at least 10 minutes.

2   Heat the coconut milk, sugar and salt in a small saucepan over a medium heat until the mixture is hot but not boiling. Slowly drop spoonfuls of the soaked gelatine into the coconut milk mixture, whisking as you go. Turn off the heat and leave to cool to room temperature.

3   Blitz the mango chunks in a food processor or blender until you have a smooth purée. Strain through a sieve, into a bowl, discarding any fibrous bits caught in the sieve. Stir the cold coconut milk mixture into the mango purée, then spoon the pudding into individual ramekins, cover with cling film and chill for at least 2 hours before serving.

4   To serve, drizzle over a generous spoonful of coconut milk, pile fresh mango cubes on top of the puddings and decorate with a sprightly sprig of mint, if you wish. Marvellous.

**Serves 4**
*3¼ tsp gelatine powder*
*250ml coconut milk, plus extra to serve*
*3 tbsp granulated sugar*
*generous pinch salt*
*2 large just-ripe mangoes (about 440g), peeled, stoned and cut into chunks or the same quantity of canned mango*
*1 ripe mango, peeled and cubed (optional)*
*few sprigs fresh mint, to serve (optional)*

There are times when only a pancake will do. Whenever you find yourself in such a position, think about turning to these gems with their crunchy filling of peanuts, coconut, sugar and sesame seeds – perfect partners for the supple yet crispy pancake. Scale up the recipe as you like but we do suggest using a large frying pan so the pancake can be rolled up in the traditional way.

# sweet sticky-filled pancake

1   In a bowl, whisk together the flours, 90ml water, milk and ½ teaspoon oil into a runny batter.

2   Heat ½ tablespoon oil in a large frying pan (at least 30cm wide) over a medium heat. Pour in the batter and use the back of a spoon to spread it out evenly into a circle. Cook for 5 minutes, until the surface has dried out and the bottom is blistered and mottled with golden yellow. Flip and cook the other side for a further 2 minutes. For extra crispiness, drizzle oil around the edge of the pancake while it is cooking, then give it a few spins in the pan to let the oil coat the bottom of the pancake.

3   Transfer the pancake to a plate so that the first side you cooked is on the bottom. Sprinkle over the filling ingredients then fold the two opposite sides of the pancake towards the centre, as if you are closing a pair of double doors, then fold in half lengthways again. Cut the rolled pancake along its length into wide slices, and eat immediately while warm and crispy.

**Makes 1**
*70g glutinous rice flour*
*1 tbsp rice flour*
*1 tbsp full-fat milk*
*½ tsp vegetable oil, plus extra for cooking*

**for the filling**
*1 tbsp granulated sugar*
*1 tbsp roasted salted peanuts, finely chopped*
*½ tbsp desiccated coconut*
*½ tbsp toasted sesame seeds*

Served in a sweet broth, these dumplings are made from a pillow-soft casing of glutinous rice flour that has a *daan gnaa* mouthfeel: a springy bite that lets you sink your teeth satisfyingly into the dumpling without it being so chewy that it sticks to your front teeth. They are traditionally filled with sweet red bean paste but the options are limitless, so feel free to experiment.

# glutinous rice dessert dumplings

1  Make the dough. Put the rice flour and sesame seeds into a large bowl, pour in 100ml water and stir vigorously until it comes together. Use your hands to squeeze the dough until it feels firm and smooth. In a separate bowl, have ready the filling ingredients.

2  To form the dumplings, take a ping-pong ball-sized piece of dough and flatten it in your palm to form a patty, then using your thumbs, apply pressure in the centre to create a bowl. Aim for the edges of the bowl to be a slightly thinner than the base.

3  Place a heaped teaspoon of filling in the base of the pre-formed bowl and bring the edges of the bowl in towards the centre, closing up the bowl as you do so. Squeeze the edges together to seal. Gently roll the dough between the palms of your hands until it is a smooth, dimple-free sphere. Repeat with the remaining dough.

4  For the ginger broth, combine the ginger and sugar with 750ml hot water in a small saucepan. Cover and simmer over a low heat for at least 10 minutes.

5  To cook the dumplings, fill a large saucepan two-thirds with hot water and bring to a rolling boil. Gently slide the dumplings into the water, then use a ladle to loosen them so they don't stick to the base of the pan. Cook for 3–4 minutes on a rolling boil until the dumplings rise to the top, then remove with a slotted spoon and serve in bowls along with a ladleful of ginger broth.

**Serves 4**

**for the dough**
*125g glutinous rice flour*
*½ tbsp black sesame seeds*

**for the filling**
*3–4 tbsp sweet red bean paste or same quantity or chocolate hazelnut spread (such as Nutella) or strawberry jam or peanut butter mixed with 1 tbsp granulated sugar*

**for the ginger broth**
*4 slices ginger*
*granulated sugar, to taste*

Buttery, creamy caramel with a secret ingredient: light soy sauce. Taking the place of salt in a traditional salted caramel sauce, the soy sauce imparts a rich umami flavour and deep copper colour that will have you dipping in time and again.

# soy salted caramel sauce

1   Heat the sugar in a medium saucepan over a medium-low heat. When a light gold ring of melted sugar starts to form around the outer edges of the pan, gently stir with a heat-proof spatula until the melted sugar is evenly distributed throughout the remaining sugar crystals. Keep stirring every 30 seconds to ensure even melting. If you find that clumps form, reduce the heat and let the sugar melt again slowly. Keep cooking for about 10 minutes until the melted sugar turns dark copper in colour.

2   Carefully add the butter and whisk quickly; the mixture will foam up at this point. Remove from the heat, add the cream and whisk until the foam settles. Leave to cool.

3   Mix in the soy sauce, a little at a time, tasting and adjusting the flavour as you go. Transfer to a lidded jar for storage. The sauce will keep in the fridge for two weeks and is delicious served with the Deep-fried Ice Cream, page opposite.

**Makes about 330ml**

*200g granulated sugar*

*90g unsalted butter, diced, at room temperature*

*160ml double cream, at room temperature*

*1½ tbsp light soy sauce*

The most joyous thing about this pudding is that in principle it reads like the ultimate oxymoron: a frozen dessert thrown into roaring hot oil. The *cheow* (crispy) coating is incredibly *houng* (fragrant) whether you opt for a cornflake crust that tastes of honey or a nutty sesame crust. Prepare your globes in advance so they are seriously frozen at the time of frying.

# deep-fried ice cream

1  Prepare the ice cream globes the night before. Quickly scoop out six tennis ball-sized globes of ice cream and arrange them on a baking sheet. Cover with cling film and re-freeze for at least 2 hours.

2  Combine the ingredients for either the cornflake or sesame seed variation in a bowl. Beat the egg and milk together in a shallow bowl.

3  Work on one globe at a time, leaving the others in the freezer. Use a rubber spatula to wedge the globe off the sheet and, working quickly, pop the globe into the dry coating mix. Use your hands to quickly pat the coating all over the globe, roll it in the egg-milk mixture then the dry mixture until the globe is completely covered. Toss it gently between your hands for a few seconds in the same way that you would toss a tennis ball – this will help shape it into a sphere. Return the coated globe to the freezer and repeat with the remaining globes. Freeze the globes overnight.

4  Heat enough oil for deep-frying in a large saucepan until you can see wisps of smoke rising from the surface. If using a deep-fryer, set the temperature to 180°C/350°F. Nestle one globe in a metal slotted spoon and carefully lower it into the oil. Use the spoon to keep the globe spinning in the oil for about 10 seconds until the coating is golden brown then remove and leave to drain on a plate lined with kitchen paper. Serve immediately because, well . . . ice cream melts!

Makes 6

*1 litre good-quality ice cream, flavour of choice*
*1 egg*
*1 tsp full-fat milk*
*vegetable oil, for deep-frying*

**for the cornflake variation**

*80g cornflakes, crushed into medium crumbs*
*80g fine breadcrumbs*

**for the sesame seed variation**

*60g sesame seeds*
*180g fine dried breadcrumbs*

In an age when big tubs of ice cream are readily available in every flavour imaginable, it's still lots of fun to make your own. Although ice cream is not a typical sweet in China, we grew up eating some of the best stuff in the world made from fresh New Zealand cream. In this 'no-churn' recipe, we infuse two of our favourite Chinese dessert flavourings into a rich custard.

# coconut and black sesame ice cream

1   Toast the sesame seeds in a small frying pan over a low heat for 5 minutes, or until they smell slightly smoky and nutty. Transfer two-thirds of the seeds to a mortar and pestle or coffee grinder and grind until they resemble cracked pepper. Mix the egg yolks and sugar together in a small bowl and set aside.

2   Heat the coconut milk gently in a small saucepan over a low heat until it is hot to the touch. Add the egg yolk mixture and vanilla and cook over a very low heat for about 10 minutes, stirring occasionally, until the mixture is thick enough to coat the back of the spoon. Pour the custard into a freezer-proof bowl and leave to cool.

3   Stir the sesame oil, ground and whole sesame seeds into the cooled custard. Whip the cream to soft peaks, then add this to the custard mixture and beat with a wooden spoon until smooth and creamy. Cover with cling film and freeze for 30 minutes.

4   Fetch the custard mixture from the freezer and vigorously beat it with a wooden spoon to get rid of any ice crystals. Return to the freezer for a further 30 minutes, before repeating the beating and returning to the freezer for another 30 minutes.

5   Beat the ice cream once more, then transfer it to a freezer-proof container. Smooth over the top, then cover and freeze for a further 2–3 hours before serving. Allow the ice cream to soften at room temperature for 5–10 minutes before eating.

Serves 4

*1½ tbsp black sesame seeds*
*3 egg yolks*
*90g granulated sugar*
*165ml coconut milk*
*½ tsp vanilla extract*
*½ tsp sesame oil*
*150ml double cream*

Courtesy of an enzyme in ginger called zingibain (what a fantastic name), a mixture of just milk and ginger magically transforms into a set pudding. Look for 'old' fibrous ginger that produces plenty of white starch when juiced. Be warned: the innocent appearance of this pudding belies its intensely fiery flavour.

# ginger milk pudding

1   Use a fine grater, food processor or blender to process the ginger into a rough pulp. Use the back of a spoon to squeeze the juice from the pulp through a fine-meshed sieve until you have collected 4 teaspoons of juice. Divide the juice between two 200ml bowls (teacups also work well). Leave for a few minutes, then tilt the bowl slightly to check that a layer of white starch has settled in the bottom. If there is no starch, the milk won't coagulate.

2   Warm the milk and sugar in a small saucepan over a low heat, stirring gently until it just starts to release steam. The milk should feel hot to the touch, but not too hot to dip your finger into. If you have a thermometer, the milk is ready when it reaches 80°C/176°F. Stir the ginger juice to evenly distribute the starch before pouring in the milk from a height of about 20cm, in one continuous stream – don't be tempted to stir. Leave to set for 5 minutes at room temperature, then eat warm or enjoy chilled.

**Serves 2**
*6–7cm piece old, fibrous ginger, peeled*
*250ml full-fat milk*
*2 tsp granulated sugar*

A good, proper stock can be the vital base ingredient that makes a dish feel extra lush and full-bodied. Making your own Cantonese-style stock is very easy and satisfying. Like all stock this one can be made ahead of time, cooled and then frozen ready for future use.

# stock

**Makes about 1.5 litres**

*500g raw bones, excess fat and skin removed (chicken carcass, pork ribs)*
*3 slices ginger*

1   Rinse the bones under cold running water, giving them a little squeeze and rub in order to coax out as much of the blood as possible. Add the rinsed bones to a large stockpot together with just enough hot water to cover them. Boil vigorously over a high heat for 5 minutes then discard the water. This 'first boil' step will make for a much cleaner and clearer stock. For an extra clear end product, rinse the boiled bones under cold water once more.

2   Add 2 litres hot water and the ginger slices to the stockpot then bring to a rapid boil over a high heat. Reduce the heat to a gentle rolling boil, cover and cook for at least 2 hours. Remove from the heat.

3   Drain the stock by pouring it through a sieve placed over a jug, a saucepan or a storage container. If you feel that your stock is too oily, simply leave it to cool after being drained, chill in the fridge, then use a spoon to skim off any excess fat that sets on the surface. Use your stock within two or three days if you are keeping it in the fridge and within two months if freezing.

If a meal calls for steamed rice, we look no further than jasmine. The tender and delicately perfumed grains of cooked jasmine rice are unbeatable vehicles for any accompaniment, and adding something as simple as a mottled drizzle of light soy sauce can make for the most satisfying meal. If you become as fanatical about rice as we are, you will discover that the freshest and tastiest rice is cooked from raw grains that gleam with natural oils.

# jasmine rice

**Serves 4**

*400g jasmine rice*

1   Put the rice into a large saucepan and cover with water. Use your hands to agitate the rice to encourage the starchy powders to detach from the grains: the water will immediately turn cloudy. Drain the water away by pouring it carefully out of the saucepan, using a cupped hand under the stream of water to catch any escapees. Keep rinsing and draining a few times until the water is almost transparent and only has the slightest hint of milkiness. Drain.

2   Pour 700ml boiling water into the saucepan and bring to the boil over a high heat. Cook, uncovered, until the surface of the rice is dotted with little craters and is almost dry. Reduce the heat to low, cover and cook for 10–15 minutes until the water has been completely absorbed. Use a fork to fluff up the rice to loosen the grains before serving.

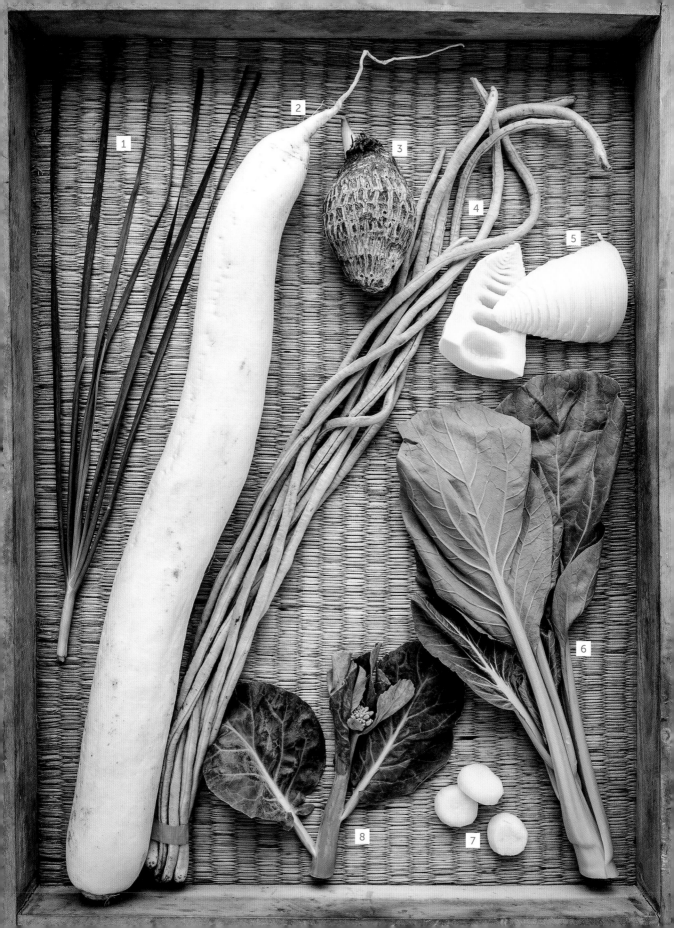

# INGREDIENTS

## VEGETABLES

### BAMBOO SHOOTS (jook shuun) 竹笋
Bamboo shoots are harvested from the cone-shaped stems that emerge from the ground when the plant is young. The firm, milky yellow flesh has a delicate perfume and is fantastic at absorbing strong flavours. Pre-sliced, canned bamboo shoots are found in large supermarkets, but try to find the whole or halved versions because they are less fibrous in texture. [5]

### CHINESE BROCCOLI (gai lan) 芥兰
*Gai lan* have tiny green flower buds and deep-emerald leaves that grow from a central stem. Its delicate bitterness is a great match for ginger, rice wine and a sprinkle of sugar in stir-fries. Avoid choosing *gai lan* with very thick and hollow stems, open flowers or yellow leaves, as these are signs of age. Fun fact: broccolini is a hybrid between broccoli and *gai lan*. [8]

### CHINESE LEAF CABBAGE (wong ah bak) 芽白
*Wong ah bak*, with their creamy white stalks and crinkly pale green leaves, are widely available in supermarkets. They are crisp and slightly sweet, and very juicy when cooked properly. Choose a cabbage free of any black or brown spots on the stalks.

### CHINESE WHITE RADISH (loh bak) 罗卜
Also known as mooli, this radish looks like a very large, pointed white carrot and its crisp, creamy white flesh has a slight peppery flavour. Choose firm radishes and check that there is only one layer of skin (Japanese daikon has two layers and has a slightly different flavour). [2]

### CHOI SUM (choy suum) 菜心
This vibrant green vegetable looks a bit like *gai lan* but tastes more like pak choi. Its sweet, juicy stems and tender leaves are delicious stir-fried or simply blanched with a drizzle of sesame oil. Choi sum are recognisable by their little yellow flowers, but choose a bunch that is still in bud for freshness. [6]

### PAK CHOI (baak choy) 白菜
The term pak choi encompasses many varieties but all of them have thick, sweet juicy stems and light to dark green leaves. The variety pak choi most commonly found in supermarkets is tall and pale green throughout.

### TARO (warh teoh) 芋头
Taro is a starchy root vegetable eaten for its unique chestnutty, coconutty flavour and floury texture. The skin is dark brown and hairy and its firm white flesh turns a ruddy lavender when cooked. Wear rubbers gloves while peeling fresh taro because it causes itchiness. Pre-sliced frozen taro is more affordable. [3]

### WATER SPINACH (tong choi, ong choi) 通菜
Harvested *tong choi* are about 40cm long and each plant features an elegant tubular stem topped with skinny, spear-shaped pointed leaves. The stem is usually cut into chopstickable pieces, which are delightfully crunchy when stir-fried, while the leaves wilt down like spinach.

### WATER CHESTNUT (marh teay) 马蹄
Water chestnuts are eaten for their *song* (refreshingly crisp) white flesh. Try sneaking little nuggets into meatballs for a surprising crunch. You can find fresh water chestnuts at the Chinese supermarket but the canned version is perfectly fine for our recipes. [7]

### YARD-LONG BEANS (dou gok) 豆角
These long, rope-like green beans have brown blemishes and retain a hearty, crunchy bite when cooked. Trim the ends before cooking. Green beans are a good substitute but reduce the cooking times. [4]

## AROMATICS

### CORIANDER (yeen say) 芫茜
Readily available in supermarkets, coriander is used in soups, stir-fries and as a garnish. Keep coriander fresher for longer in the fridge by wrapping in damp kitchen paper followed by a plastic bag.

### GARLIC (shuhn towh) 蒜头
You know this one. We are not too fussy about our garlic but do try to buy only as much as we need because the bulbs dry out easily.

### GARLIC CHIVES (gowh choi) 韭菜
The slender green blades have a distinct garlicky flavour that is delicious when stir-fried. You will find them as tied bunches or in sealed plastic bags in Chinese supermarkets: avoid if the tips look burnished or yellow, as these are signs of age. [1]

### GINGER (saang gheung) 生姜
Choose firm, knobbly looking ginger with rough tan skin and fibrous flesh. Smooth-skinned ginger tends to have more fibres and less flavour. This is not to be confused with 'young' ginger, which has smooth skin and pink tips.

### SPRING ONION (cong) 葱

A true staple of Cantonese cooking, spring onions are used almost everywhere: to flavour oils and add depth to braises, in dumpling fillings, or as a garnish. The bunches in supermarkets usually have their pointed ends chopped off so add more than the recipe calls for if you like – it's not a precise science.

## TOFU

### TOFU (dou fu) 豆腐

Tofu comes in different degrees of firmness: silken, soft, firm and extra-firm. The soft kind is what you are looking for when making braises such as Mapo Tofu (page 100), while the firm kinds are good for pan-frying. Store in the fridge covered in water.  10

### FRIED TOFU (jaa dou fu) 炸豆腐

Deep-frying tofu turns it into the most wondrous sponge for other flavours. Cubes of deep-fried tofu are sold in packets in the fridge in Chinese supermarkets: use quickly as they will go mouldy within a few days.  14

## PRESERVED AND FERMENTED

### FERMENTED BLACK BEANS (douchi) 豆豉

These wrinkly looking beans have a sharp, pungent umami flavour that pack a lot of punch. They are also intensely salty so rinse them first, use sparingly and with a sprinkling of sugar. You will find them sold in vacuum-sealed bags or in cardboard tubes in Chinese supermarkets.  20

## SAUCES AND PASTES

### CHILLI BEAN SAUCE (dou ban jeung) 豆瓣酱

A spicy, salty paste made from fermented chilli and broad beans often used in Sichuan cooking. The most authentic versions are from the town of Pixian and contain large pieces of chilli and broad beans that should be chopped roughly before using. Fry the paste in hot oil to release its ruby red oils.  13

### HOISIN SAUCE (hoy seen jeung) 海鲜酱

Hoisin sauce is savoury, sweet and tangy all at once and used in stir-fries, sauces and for dipping. The colour will vary from dark chocolate to a reddish brown (if it contains red fermented rice). Avoid hoisins the colour of milk chocolate as this suggests a heavy use of thickeners. As for texture, the best hoisin sauces should be scoopable (like soft ice cream) and definitely not runny.

### OYSTER SAUCE (hoh yeoh) 蚝油

Oyster sauce is traditionally made by simmering fresh oysters in water until they caramelise to a viscous and intensely flavoured sauce. The versions available now use oyster extract or essence. Use for glazing a stir-fry, dolloped on top of blanched greens or simply mixed through noodles.

### RED BEAN PASTE (hong dou shaa) 豆沙

Made from mashed azuki beans, the paste is honey-sweet, velvety smooth and good enough to eat with a spoon. Find in cans or vacuum-sealed bags in Chinese supermarkets.  15

### SHA CHA SAUCE 沙茶酱

Sha cha is an intensely savoury and slightly spicy sauce made from an aromatic combination of garlic, shallots, chilli and dried shrimp. The paste separates from the oil, so stir thoroughly before using. You can use it as a marinade, braising sauce, barbecue rub or condiment for noodles.

### SOY SAUCE (see yeoh: sarng cheo, lhoh cheo) 豉油: 生抽, 老抽

The two types of soy sauce most widely used in the Chinese kitchen are light and dark soy. Light soy (sarng cheo) is the saltier of the two and is used for flavour and seasoning. Dark soy (lhoh cheo) is fermented from light soy and has a mellower flavour and is deeper in colour and added during cooking. A good dark soy will coat the inside of a glass bottle when inverted while a runny consistency is a sign of poor quality. If you are gluten intolerant go for tamari, a Japanese soy sauce made with little or no wheat (check the bottle).

### SWEET BEAN SAUCE (tem meen jeung) 甜面酱

Sweet bean sauce is made from fermented wheat, salt and soybeans and is the thick, glossy sauce nestled inside Peking duck pancakes. Since it is also sold as sweet fermented sauce, sweet flour sauce and hoisin sauce (which it is not, although they are good substitutes for each other), be sure to show the Chinese characters to a shop assistant.  11

### YELLOW SOYBEAN PASTE (wong jeung) 黄酱

The name describes the yellow soybeans used to make the sauce as, once fermented, the paste is light to dark brown colour. It is primarily used in Northern Chinese cuisine to add umami richness to dishes. A drier version, called ghon wong jeung (literally 'dry yellow paste') is also available in Chinese supermarkets.  12

## SEEDS, SPICES AND CHILLI

### SESAME SEEDS (zi maa) 芝麻

The inviting aroma of freshly toasted sesame seeds can really lift a dish. Black sesame seeds, on the other hand, can add graphic impact but are less pleasant to eat as the hulls are gritty. For both, store in an airtight container to stop the seeds from going rancid.

## STAR ANISE (baat gok) 八角

These eight-pointed star-shaped dried fruits have a strong aniseed flavour and are used sparingly in braises and stews where their fragrance can permeate sauces. 19

## FIVE-SPICE POWDER (ng heung fun) 五香粉

This spice blend typically consists of ground cloves, star anise, cinnamon, Sichuan pepper and fennel seeds, although recipes vary and can include components such as ginger and mandarin peel. The pungent, heavily aromatic powder is often paired with fatty meats like pork and duck. To create a delicious seasoned salt for finishing off dishes, simply dry-roast equal portions of five-spice and table salt in a hot saucepan and store in an airtight container.

## SICHUAN PEPPER (faa jiew) 花椒

'Flower pepper' in Chinese, Sichuan 'peppercorns' are actually dried berries. They are usually sold cracked open like ladybird wings with the seeds discarded, since it is the woody husk that induces the tingly, numbing sensation on the tongue. They can be added whole in braises or roasted and then freshly ground before use. When used alongside chillies, the effect is called *maa laat*, literally 'numb-spicy'. 21

## WHITE PEPPER (bak wu jiew) 白胡椒

This is more often than not the pepper of choice for Chinese cooks because it won't mottle the appearance of light-coloured dishes as black pepper can.

## OILS

### SESAME OIL (zi maa yeoh) 芝麻油

Sesame oil is used as a flavour enhancer, not a cooking oil, and as such should be added at the end of cooking. This is also because the flavour molecules in sesame oil are very delicate and are destroyed by heat. Look for 'pure' sesame oil, which has not been blended with other oils (and is not that much more expensive than the blended varieties).

### LARD AND VEGETABLE SHORTENING (ju yeoh) 猪油

Although out of fashion, lard is an integral ingredient in many traditional Chinese baked breads and pastries as it creates a tender crumb and well-defined layers. On the whole, lard is not interchangeable with butter as the constitution is very different but vegetable shortening (look for 100 per cent vegetable fat) can be substituted.

## RICE WINE AND VINEGAR

### SHAOXING RICE WINE (siew hing jiao) 绍兴酒

Made from glutinous rice, this dark amber liquid is used to add depth to marinades and an unmistakable fragrance to stir-fries. It is not good for drinking. Supermarkets stock Shaoxing rice wine in small bottles but try to get your hands on a more authentic version in the Chinese supermarket if you can. Avoid 'cooking wine', which is salted and entirely different. Dry sherry is a good substitute. 17

### CHINKIANG VINEGAR (jun ghong hohng chouw) 镇江香醋

This mildly acidic vinegar from the city of Zhenjiang (formerly Chinkiang) has an almost smoky flavour. It is used as a dipping sauce for dumplings (especially those with fatty fillings) and added at the start of braises to intensify flavour. At a pinch, you could substitute with equal parts balsamic and water. 9

## DRIED GOODS

### DRIED CHINESE MUSHROOMS OR SHIITAKE (dong gu) 冬菇

Good dried Chinese mushrooms can have the pungency of dried porcini, only less earthy and more perfumed. The lighter-coloured mushrooms with lots of tiny cracks on their caps are the most prized (and accordingly priced) for their intensity of flavour. To prepare them for cooking, soak in hot water with a pinch of sugar (to counter any bitterness) for 30 minutes. They are eaten for their fleshy caps, but you can break off the stalks before soaking to use in stocks. 16

### LOTUS LEAVES (hhoh yep) 荷叶

Lotus leaves are used as wrappers to imbue a delicate floral fragrance to their contents, such as glutinous rice (see Steamed Lotus Leaf Parcels, page 48). They need a rinse and soak in lukewarm water before use. 22

### SNOW EAR (shurt yee) 雪耳

Snow ear is a tree fungus that is wondrously *song* (refreshingly crisp) in texture when cooked and will lap up sauces within its overlapping fronds. It is particularly delicious when simmered in a hoisin-based sauce. Cut off any tough knobbly bits at the base and soak in cold water for 10 minutes, after which they will expand to about three times the size. Also called silver ear fungus or white jelly mushroom. 18

## FLOURS AND STARCHES

### LOW-PROTEIN FLOUR *(day gun fun)* 低筋粉
Containing only 8–10 per cent protein, the low elasticity of this flour is suitable for making pillowy soft breads such as in Steamed Pork Buns (page 40). The fine milling process also produces a whiter flour than plain flour (10–12 per cent protein), although it is not as snowy white as the bleached flour used in China and Hong Kong (unavailable in the UK). Buy it in the Chinese supermarket or online, where it is sometimes called 'dim sum flour'. 28

### RICE FLOUR *(jee mei fun)* 粘米粉
A flour made from finely ground long-grain rice used in steamed sweet and savoury cakes, such as the Pan-fried Turnip Cake (page 34). Add a touch of rice flour to a glutinous rice flour dough if you want it to crisp up when fried (otherwise it remains tender and soft). 25

### GLUTINOUS RICE FLOUR *(lo meen fun)* 糯米粉
Milled from glutinous rice, this flour produces a flexible, resilient dough that imparts a sticky, chewy texture to sweet snacks and desserts. It is not interchangeable with rice flour. 23

### TAPIOCA STARCH *(ling fun)* 菱粉
A starchy powder extracted from the root vegetable cassava that is used as a thickener in the same way as cornflour. It is sometimes called tapioca flour, although it is gluten-free. Fun fact: the chewy, translucent balls in bubble tea are tapioca pearls. 27

### WHEAT STARCH *(dung meen fun)* 澄面粉
The starchy part of wheat only (no gluten) ground into a fine powder. It is essential for achieving the pliable, translucent wrappers of the delicately steamed Prawn Claw Dumplings (page 25). 24

### AMMONIUM BICARBONATE *(cheoh fun)* 臭粉
A predecessor to the modern raising agents bicarbonate of soda and baking powder, ammonium bicarbonate is still used in Chinese cooking for its ability to produce more gas for the same amount of agent without leaving a soapy taste. The powder has a strong ammonia smell, which must be cooked off completely, so only small amounts should be used. It is easy to source online as food grade ammonium bicarbonate. 26

## WRAPPERS

### WONTON WRAPPERS *(won ton pei)* 云吞皮
These silky wrappers are made from wheat flour, water and egg and are sold frozen or chilled in the Chinese supermarket. When you have a choice, use the thinner wrappers for steaming and boiling, and the thicker wrappers for deep-frying (check the label). You can sometimes find round versions for Pork and Prawn Open Dumplings (page 20). 29

### SPRING ROLL WRAPPERS *(chun gurn pei)* 春卷皮
These are simply larger versions of wonton wrappers and if you can find them, the best kind for deep-frying contain no egg and are almost translucent (sometimes called 'Shanghai spring roll wrappers').

## RICE AND NOODLES

### JASMINE RICE *(heung mei)* 香米
Mostly grown in Thailand, the nutty, fragrant, tender and ever so sticky jasmine rice is the best choice for steaming, in our opinion. The best-quality jasmine rice will leach a little oil as it cooks: a sign that it hasn't been stored for a long time. 30

### LONG-GRAIN RICE *(cheung meii)* 长米
Ideal for fried rice as the cooked grains are more robust than jasmine rice.

### GLUTINOUS RICE *(law mei)* 糯米
When cooked, the grains are tacky and translucent with a firm bite. Prepare by washing then soaking overnight and steam over a rapid boil for the best results. 35

### BEAN THREAD VERMICELLI *(fun see)* 粉丝
Also known as cellophane noodles or glass noodles, these long resilient threads are made from ground mung beans. They are ready to cook after a soak in cold water and once cooked, are a bit gelatinous and supremely *waat* (slippery). They soak up flavours like a sponge so are best used in saucy dishes. 31

### FRESH WONTON NOODLES *(won ton meen)* 吞面
Some Chinese supermarkets stock fresh wonton noodles in the fridge. These are more elastic than ordinary egg noodles and more closely resemble the kind that you would find in a wonton noodle shop in Hong Kong. 33

### RICE NOODLES *(mei fun, sa ho fun)* 米粉, 沙河粉
The two types used in Chinese cooking are *mei fun* (super-skinny) and *sa ho fun* (flat and wide). Soak both types in cold water until floppy then briefly boil until supple just before eating. 32 34

### WHEAT NOODLES *(meen)* 面
Made with or without egg, sold fresh or dried, these are the most common type of noodles used in Chinese cooking.

# OUR GO-TO CHINESE SUPPLIERS

Thanks to a growing eagerness to cook Chinese food at home, you will easily find most of the ingredients in the supermarket. Everything else can be picked up at any good Chinese supermarket, some of which we have recommended here. If it's your first visit, we encourage you to take this book with you and use the Chinese characters in the glossary to help you find the right item.

## LONDON'S CHINATOWN

### NEW LOON MOON
9A Gerrard St, London W1D 5PN

Scores top points from us with its great selection of products and wide aisles for comfortable browsing. Don't forget to explore the first floor where you will find dried goods (including many of our 'add an exotic' ingredients) and plenty of candy-coated treats.

### SEEWOO
18–20 Lisle St, London WC2H 7BE

The best part of this shop is the Aladdin's cave of kitchen equipment in the basement, where you will find everything from woks to a special pig skin pricker for making five-spiced roast pork belly (we think bamboo skewers do the trick). They also have branches in Glasgow and Greenwich.

### LOON FUNG
42–44 Gerrard Street, London W1D 5QG

The owners have managed to pack a lot of stock into the space, so you are sure to find what you are after. There are three other branches dotted around London.

## ONLINE

We have found that prices online are no different than at brick-and-mortar shops but the shopping experience can vary greatly. After analysing each site by product selection, user-friendliness and searchability, here are our top picks:

### www.waiyeehong.com

The fantastic selection of products is well categorised and the detailed product descriptions include helpful Chinese characters. The autofill function in the search box (which makes suggestions based on the product listing used on the site) is handy if you're not sure about brandnames or descriptions.

### www.tradewindsorientalshop.co.uk

The site is well organised with sensible product categories and the selection is impressive considering that they also stock Caribbean, Filipino, Korean, Japanese, Thai and Vietnamese products.

### www.orientaltreasure.co.uk

We like the detailed product descriptions along with their helpful recipe suggestions.

# INDEX

## Acknowledgements

Our wonderful editor and fellow Kiwi, Kate, summed it up the best during one of our earliest meetings at Orion house:

'It's like a baby: you work hard on it, it's kind of gone for a few months while it is printing . . . and then before you know it, all of a sudden, it arrives!'

It is quite apt to compare the experience of writing our first Dumpling cookbook to having a proverbial bun in the oven. Reaching major milestones was exhilarating, we had a few wobbly moments along the way, and all the while we remained buoyed by anticipation for the day that our hearts would swell with pride when we finally got to hold this special thing in our hands.

Although we run the risk of overusing the analogy and inducing some rather interesting imagery, we want to acknowledge that our baby would not have been possible without the nurturing support, talent and determination of a brilliant bunch of people who are well and truly a part of our Dumpling Family.

Without further ado, we'd like to say a ma-hoosive thanks to . . .

Amanda Harris at Orion Publishing, for first spotting us at a time when most of our YouTube views still came from Mum and Dad. Kate Wanwimolruk, editor extraordinaire, for your expertise, patience, passion and understanding. You're one of the kindest and most hilarious people we know. Kathy Steer, for masterfully copy-editing our book into shape.

Thanks to the creative team including Sara Griffin and Lucie Stericker. Paul Winch-Furness, a trillion thanks for your eye-wateringly stunning photography (and for those eye-watering mega sour sweets). Cheers also to Jake and Jay for the abundance of laughs during shoots and for your expert reflector skills. Olivia Wardle, where would we be without your ridiculously good propping eye? You knew what we loved before we did! Thanks to Henrietta Clancy, epic food styler and inspiration behind the phrase that still pops into mind every time we plate up: 'what would Hen do?'. Gabriella Le Grazie, thanks for your superhuman ability to interpret and decipher everyone's visions in order to produce a wonderful design that we're all in love with. Thanks also to Ellis Parrinder, Ellie Lines, and Irena Rogers, for practising your crafts with us on location day.

To the sales, marketing, and publicity crew at Orion, including Mark McGinlay and Alice Morley: thanks for working so hard to help us get our baby out into the world!

To our superbly sassy literary agent, Ariella 'Sweet Pants' Feiner, thanks for your unwavering and indispensable support. You always give us confidence that in the end, *everything* will turn out awesome. A big thanks also to Rosemary Scoular and Aoife Rice at United Agents.

Friends and followers, both new and old, both near and far: we simply cannot thank you enough for all your Facebook 'likes', enthusiastic feedback and proud food photos that give us some serious warm fuzzies. We hope that this book delights your tastebuds and gets a good workout on your kitchen bench.

And finally, Dad, Mum, and Justin: thanks for being you. Oh, and also for that little thing where you divulged all of your cooking secrets to us so that we could go forth and share them with the world. But seriously, this book is as much yours as it is ours.

Sending galactic-sized love to everyone,

*A&J x*